Contents

How to use this book

Yellow boxes give you useful tips to help you understand the questions.

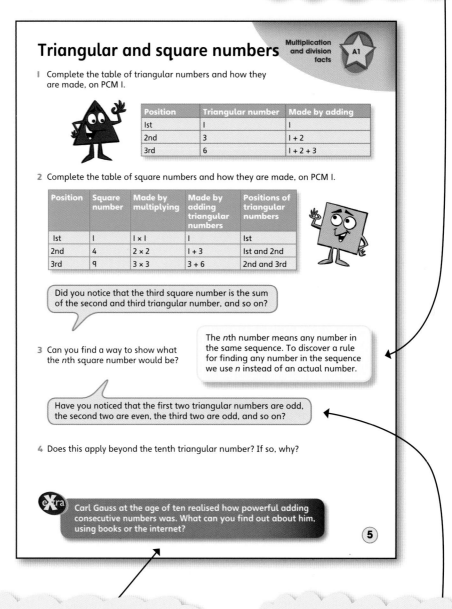

Triangular and square numbers

Multiplication and division facts — A1

1 Complete the table of triangular numbers and how they are made, on PCM 1.

Position	Triangular number	Made by adding
1st	1	1
2nd	3	1 + 2
3rd	6	1 + 2 + 3

2 Complete the table of square numbers and how they are made, on PCM 1.

Position	Square number	Made by multiplying	Made by adding triangular numbers	Positions of triangular numbers
1st	1	1 × 1	1	1st
2nd	4	2 × 2	1 + 3	1st and 2nd
3rd	9	3 × 3	3 + 6	2nd and 3rd

Did you notice that the third square number is the sum of the second and third triangular number, and so on?

3 Can you find a way to show what the nth square number would be?

The nth number means any number in the same sequence. To discover a rule for finding any number in the sequence we use n instead of an actual number.

Have you noticed that the first two triangular numbers are odd, the second two are even, the third two are odd, and so on?

4 Does this apply beyond the tenth triangular number? If so, why?

eXtra Carl Gauss at the age of ten realised how powerful adding consecutive numbers was. What can you find out about him, using books or the internet?

5

If you finish the main activity before the end of the lesson, you can move on to the Extra activity.

Speech bubbles raise interesting questions that you can discuss with others in your group.

Very large numbers

Here are the standard names for some very large numbers.

Name	In figures		Factor
one	1		10^0
ten	10		10^1
hundred	100		10^2
thousand	1000		10^3
million	1 000 000		10^6
billion	1 000 000 000		10^9
trillion	1 000 000 000 000		10^{12}
quadrillion	1 000 000 000 000 000		10^{15}
quintillion	1 000 000 000 000 000 000		10^{18}
sextillion	1 000 000 000 000 000 000 000		10^{21}
septillion	1 000 000 000 000 000 000 000 000		10^{24}

What is a billion? What is a trillion? Do you know any other very large numbers?

But there are numbers even larger than this!

A googol is the number 10^{100}, that is, the digit 1 followed by 100 zeros:

10 000 000 000 000 000 000 000 000 000 000 000 000 000 000 000 000 000 000 000 000 0 00 000 000 000 000 000 000 000 000 000 000 000 000 000

The word googol was invented in 1920 by a nine-year-old boy called Milton Sirotta. He was the nephew of an American mathematician called Edward Kasner.

A googolplex is a very, very large number. It is much bigger than a googol times a googol! A googol times a googol is 1 with 200 zeros. A googolplex is 1 with a googol of zeros. This number is so large that you would never be able to write all the zeros. It is the second largest number with a name.

The largest number with a name is a googolplexian. This is the digit 1 followed by a googolplex of zeros.

1 How long would it take to count to a million if you counted one number a second? Time yourself counting to 100 quickly and calculate how long it might take you to count to a million.

2 To get plenty of exercise we should all walk 10 000 steps a day. Measure one of your steps and calculate how far this is.

3 A charity raises a kilometre of 10 pence pieces. See how many 10 pence pieces there are in 10 cm and work out how much a kilometre of ten pence pieces is worth. What if they were £1 coins?

Use the internet to find out how many cells there are in your body. Find out the names of some very small numbers.

Inequalities and symbols

| ≈ | ≥ | ≤ | > | < |

1 Complete the table by filling in the blank squares with the tiles shown above.

	3	6	÷	9	*a*	4				9		
						5	×	0	·4	*b*	1	0
						6				9		
				7		×				·0		
				3		7				1		
1	2	·3	4	÷	9	*c*	1	·5				
				1		3						
				0		0						
				0		0	·6	×	1	0	*d*	6
7	·3	×	3	*e*	2	0						
				0								
				·5								

Some of these statements are incorrect. Work out which ones and correct them.

2 $3·4 > 4·3$

3 $0·23 > 0·2$

4 $170 < 171 > 175$

5 $8 < 10 < 12$

6 On a number line, 4·05 lies between 4·1 and 4·5

Insert a number in place of *n* in each of these statements to make them correct.

7 $75 + n > 100$

8 $62 - 10 < n$

9 $5 < n < 7$

10 $2·0 > n > 1·0$

11 $\frac{1}{2} > n > \frac{1}{4}$

Triangular and square numbers

1 Complete the table of triangular numbers and how they are made, on PCM 1.

Position	Triangular number	Made by adding
1st	1	1
2nd	3	1 + 2
3rd	6	1 + 2 + 3

2 Complete the table of square numbers and how they are made, on PCM 1.

Position	Square number	Made by multiplying	Made by adding triangular numbers	Positions of triangular numbers
1st	1	1 × 1	1	1st
2nd	4	2 × 2	1 + 3	1st and 2nd
3rd	9	3 × 3	3 + 6	2nd and 3rd

Did you notice that the third square number is the sum of the second and third triangular number, and so on?

The *n*th number means any number in the same sequence. To discover a rule for finding any number in the sequence we use *n* instead of an actual number.

3 Can you find a way to show what the *n*th square number would be?

Have you noticed that the first two triangular numbers are odd, the second two are even, the third two are odd, and so on?

4 Does this apply beyond the tenth triangular number? If so, why?

eXtra Carl Gauss at the age of ten realised how powerful adding consecutive numbers was. What can you find out about him, using books or the internet?

Recurring decimals

We can use a calculator to find $\frac{1}{9}$ as a decimal.

Use a calculator to find the decimal equivalents of these fractions.

1 $\frac{2}{9}$ 2 $\frac{3}{9}$ 3 $\frac{4}{9}$

Without using a calculator, predict the decimal equivalents of these fractions.

4 $\frac{5}{9}$ 5 $\frac{6}{9}$ 6 $\frac{7}{9}$ 7 $\frac{8}{9}$

8 What is the decimal equivalent of $\frac{9}{9}$? What is special about this number?

Use a calculator to find the decimal equivalents of these fractions.

9 $\frac{1}{11}$ 10 $\frac{2}{11}$ 11 $\frac{3}{11}$ 12 $\frac{4}{11}$

Without using a calculator, predict the decimal equivalents of these fractions.

13 $\frac{5}{11}$ 14 $\frac{7}{11}$ 15 $\frac{8}{11}$ 16 $\frac{10}{11}$

What happens when you try this with other fraction families, such as $\frac{1}{27}$, $\frac{2}{27}$, $\frac{3}{27}$, and so on?

 e**X**tra

Use a calculator to find the decimal equivalent of $\frac{1}{7}$.
You will see

0·142857142857142857

We call this a **cyclic number**.

We can show this pattern using a diagram.

What is the decimal equivalent of $\frac{2}{7}$? $\frac{3}{7}$? What do you notice?

Can you find any more decimal equivalents that are cyclic numbers?

Equivalent fractions

> $20 \div 3 = 6\frac{2}{3}$
>
> What is $40 \div 6$?

1 What other divisions equal $6\frac{2}{3}$? Write as many as you can find.

2 How do the numbers in the divisions change? Is there a pattern?

3 Choose five mixed numbers from the list below.
   For each one, write four divisions to give that answer.

   $5\frac{1}{3}$ $4\frac{3}{5}$ $1\frac{4}{9}$

   $8\frac{5}{6}$ $4\frac{3}{4}$ $3\frac{1}{4}$

   $7\frac{1}{8}$ $2\frac{5}{7}$ $13\frac{2}{5}$

4 Describe the patterns that you have found.

> $14 \div 3 = 4\frac{2}{3}$
>
> $28 \div 6 = 4\frac{4}{6}$
>
> $\frac{2}{3}$ and $\frac{4}{6}$ are equivalent fractions, so we can cancel
> $4\frac{4}{6}$ down to $4\frac{2}{3}$ and say that $28 \div 6 = 4\frac{2}{3}$

5 Which of these fractions is equivalent to $\frac{2}{3}$? How do you know?

   $\frac{5}{7}$ $\frac{20}{30}$ $\frac{6}{9}$ $\frac{8}{12}$ $\frac{3}{4}$ $\frac{10}{15}$ $\frac{3}{5}$ $\frac{30}{45}$

6 Can you find a fraction equivalent to $\frac{2}{3}$ with the numerator 3?

eXtra

> $28 \div 3 = 9\frac{1}{3} = 9\cdot\dot{3}$

The table on PCM 4 shows other divisions
with the answer $9\cdot\dot{3}$.

Describe what strategy you will use to help you complete this table.

Complete the table on PCM 4 by filling in the missing numbers.

Multiplying and dividing even and odd numbers

> Do you remember the rules for adding and subtracting even and odd numbers?

Check by answering these questions:

36 + 22 =   48 + 27 =   35 + 19 =

36 – 22 =   48 – 27 =   35 – 19 =

> What do you think will happen when you multiply and divide odd and even numbers?

48   36

25   45

90   81

24   12

3   5

30   27

1   Choose one even number from the diamond and one even number from the circle. Multiply them together. Is the answer even or odd? Do this three more times. What do you find?

2   Repeat with an odd number from each shape. What happens this time?

3   Try with an even number from one shape and an odd number from the other shape. What do you notice?

4   Now divide even and odd numbers from the diamond by even and odd numbers from the circle. Do you get the same results as for multiplying?

5   What happens when the number from the diamond is not exactly divisible by the number from the circle?

What happens when three even numbers are multiplied together?
What happens when three odd numbers are multiplied together?
A combination of three or more even and odd numbers?

Use your calculator to explore.

Number sequences

17   19   15   17   13   15   ...

1 Will every number occur twice? Why?

2 Why are there no even numbers in this sequence?

19   28   26   30   39   37   41   50   ...

3 Which multiples of 10 come into this sequence?

4 Is there any pattern to this?

126   327   297   498   468   ...

5 How many more numbers before the sequence reaches 1000 or more?

6 How many more numbers before the sequence reaches 2000 or more?

Find the five numbers that go before and the five numbers that go after each set.

7

					2·54	2·57	2·60					

8

					⁻3·4	⁻2·9	⁻2·4					

9

					$\frac{1}{4}$	1	$1\frac{3}{4}$					

10

					6	$4\frac{3}{5}$	$3\frac{1}{5}$					

 e**X**tra Make up your own number sequences. If you have time, challenge a classmate to find the patterns.

Investigating number sequences

> **Rules**
> Start with any whole number between 10 and 100.
> If the number is even, halve it.
> If the number is odd, add 1. Halve this number.
> Continue doing this until you reach the number 1.

1 Start with the number 20, and apply the rules. Write the sequence.

2 How many steps did it take to get to 1?

3 Choose three different start numbers and write the sequences.
  How many steps did each one take?

4 Which number between 10 and 100 takes the most steps to get to 1?

> I started with 60.
> 60, 30, 15, 16, 8, 4, 2, 1.
> That's seven steps!

> I started with 53.
> 53, 54, 27, 28, 14, 7, 8, 4, 2, 1.
> That's nine steps!
> I think it's better to start with an odd number.

5 If you start with 625, it will take 16 steps to reach 1. Can you find a number below 1000 that takes more steps than this?

eXtra Try changing the rules of the sequence.
What if you added 3 rather than 1 to odd numbers?
What if you multiplied odd numbers by 3 and then added 1?

Making quadrilaterals

> How many different quadrilaterals can you make on a 3 × 3 pinboard?

Remember, rotations and reflections don't count.
For example, these two shapes count as the same shape:

Find as many unique quadrilaterals as you can. Each time you find a new one, draw it on a grid on PCM 5. Try to find at least one shape for each section of the Carroll diagram on PCM 6.

Cut out the quadrilaterals that you have found. Fill in the Carroll diagram on PCM 6 by arranging your quadrilaterals in the correct places, like this.

	Parallel sides	No parallel sides
Perpendicular sides		
No perpendicular sides		

 eXtra Make pentagons and hexagons on a 3 × 3 pinboard. Can you make at least one pentagon and one hexagon to go in each section of the Carroll diagram?

Parallel and perpendicular

Can you see any parallel edges? Parallel faces?

The Houses of Parliament, London

The Alhambra, Granada

The Louvre, Paris

The White House, Washington DC

Can you see any perpendicular edges? Perpendicular faces?

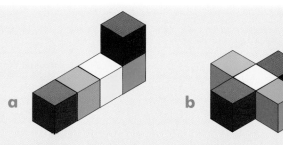

a   b

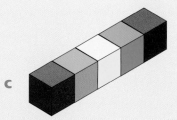

c

1 Which shape has the largest number of pairs of parallel faces?

2 Which shape has the l

How can you be sure you have counted all of the faces?

3 Find eight different ways to join five cubes.
Which gives the greatest number of parallel faces? Perpendicular faces?
Which gives the least number of parallel faces? Perpendicular faces?

e**X**tra

What arrangement of six cubes would give the maximum number of parallel faces? Perpendicular faces? How about the minimum number? What if you had seven cubes? Eight cubes? Nine cubes?

Tables and graphs

Miss Nawaz's class grew some sunflowers.

Table 1 Sunflower heights

Child	Sunflower height	Child	Sunflower height	Child	Sunflower height
Brandon	59 cm	Megan	59 cm	Daniel	60 cm
Jenna	63 cm	Toby	63 cm	Tanisha	64 cm
Rico	64 cm	Tara	58 cm	Jack	59 cm
Paige	59 cm	James	59 cm	Ella	62 cm
Ellis	61 cm	Luca	65 cm	Aku	57 cm
Vanessa	65 cm	Faraz	56 cm	Megan	61 cm
Aaliya	58 cm	Sabrina	62 cm	Caitlin	64 cm
Samuel	56 cm	George	61 cm	Hamzah	62 cm
Mia	62 cm	Phoebe	64 cm	Helena	56 cm
Andrew	65 cm	Mosi	62 cm	Jody	59 cm

1 Draw a frequency table to show this information.

2 Draw a bar graph to show this information.

Luca grew one of the tallest sunflowers.

He measured the growth of his sunflower over two weeks.

Table 2 The height of Luca's sunflower over two weeks

Day	Sunflower height	Day	Sunflower height
May 10th	14 cm	May 17th	49 cm
May 11th	16 cm	May 18th	58 cm
May 12th	19 cm	May 19th	60 cm
May 13th	23 cm	May 20th	62 cm
May 14th	28 cm	May 21st	64 cm
May 15th	34 cm	May 22nd	65 cm
May 16th	41 cm	May 23rd	65 cm

3 Draw a line graph to show this information.

Make up some questions about the graphs that you have drawn. Ask other children in your class to answer your questions by looking at the graphs.

Line graphs and conversion graphs

Table I   Population of London since 1801

Year	Population in millions (to the nearest half million)	Year	Population in millions (to the nearest half million)
1801	1	1931	8
1831	1·5	1951	8·5
1851	2·5	1971	7·5
1901	6·5	1981	7
1921	7·5	2001	7·5

The population has grown very quickly over the last 200 years.

I Is this true? Complete the line graph on PCM 8 to investigate.

2 Between which years was the population growth the quickest?

3 Predict what will happen to the population growth after 2001.

Conversion graph (mph and km/h)

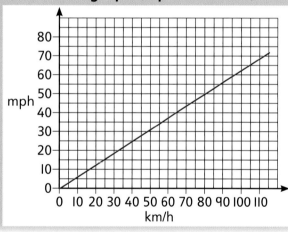

4 If Alex is driving at 30 mph, what is her approximate speed in km/h?

5 Jerome is driving at 60 mph. Is his speed in km/h exactly double Alex's speed in km/h?

6 On motorways in France the speed limit when it is raining is 110 km/h. Approximately how fast is this in mph?

Table 2   Equivalent weights in kilograms and pounds

Kilograms	0 kg	25 kg	37·5 kg	50 kg
Pounds	0 lb	55 lb	82·5 lb	110 lb

7 Draw a conversion graph for kilograms and pounds.

8 How many kg is approximately 30 pounds?

9 How many pounds is approximately 30 kg?

Use the internet to look up the change in population of another capital city. Draw a line graph to show this, and compare it to the population of London.

Averages

Table 1 Joe and Salma's maths homework scores this term

Joe	5	6	7	4	5	4	5	3	6	7
Salma	6	7	3	4	5	6	3	🐾	2	5

> Salma: The mode is the number that appears the most often.
>
> Joe: The mode is the biggest number.

1 Who is right?

2 What is the mode of Joe's scores?

3 The mode of Salma's scores is 6. What is the missing number hidden by the ink blot?

> Salma: To find the mean you just add all the numbers together.
>
> Joe: To find the mean, you add up all the numbers and divide by how many numbers there are.

4 Who is right?

5 What is the mean of Joe's scores?

6 What is the mean of Salma's scores?

> Salma: We can't find the median. We have an even amount of scores, so there are two numbers in the middle.
>
> Joe: To find the median if there are two numbers in the middle, we add them together and divide by 2.

7 Who is right?

8 What is Joe's median score?

9 What is Salma's median score?

> Salma: To find the range you take the smallest number away from the largest number.
>
> Joe: The range is the amount of scores we each have.

10 Who is right?

11 What is the range of Joe's scores?

12 What is the range of Salma's scores?

Table 2 Maths homework scores for three other children this term

Mark	3	6	5	4	5	7	8	5	6	2
Freya	9	5	7	8	3	9	9	4	6	4
Sol	8	9	5	7	8	9	8	4	5	3

13 Work out the mode, mean and median and range of each child's scores.

14 Including Salma and Joe, who did best in their maths homework? Why?

These are the scores after the first 10 overs of a cricket match. Find the mean, median, mode and range of these scores. Who played better?

Greentown Cricket Club	3	5	8	12	2	0	1	18	0	4
Bluebrooke Cricket Club	4	8	5	2	6	4	9	3	8	4

Imperial or metric?

There are two systems of measurement: imperial and metric.

Imperial measurements have been used in Britain for hundreds of years.

The metric system was adopted in France in 1795, and is now used worldwide.

Its basic units are metres, litres and grams.

In 1995 it became law for people in Britain to use metric measurements for most things, but not everything.

> Can you think of any examples of places where you can still see imperial units of measurement?

Foot	Created by the Romans, based on the length of a person's foot. There are 12 inches in a foot.
Yard	From the Anglo-Saxon word *gyrd* which means 'stick'. Sticks were used for measuring before people had rulers. There are 3 feet in a yard.
Mile	From the Latin word *mille* which means 1000, because it was equal to 1000 paces. There are 1760 yards in a mile.
Ounce	From the Latin word *uncia* which means 'one twelfth'. The abbreviation *oz* comes from the Italian word *onza*. There are 16 ounces in a pound.
Pound	From the Latin word *pendere* which means 'to weigh'. The abbreviation *lb* comes from the Latin *libra* which means weighing scales. There are 14 pounds in a stone.
Pint	This may have come from the Latin word *picta* meaning 'painted', because people painted a line on a jug to mark how much a pint was. There are 8 pints in a gallon.

> When do we use imperial units to measure? When do we use metric?

⏸ Find some containers and bottles around the classroom, and make a note of their weights or capacities. What do you notice? Do you think it is easy to buy ingredients for a recipe? Is it easy to compare the costs of ingredients?

e**X**tra Do your parents give their height and weight in imperial or metric units of measurement? What do you use?
Find out how to convert your height and weight into imperial if you use metric, or metric if you use imperial.

Rectangles and rhombuses

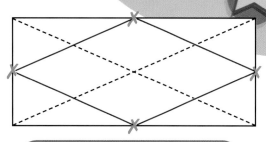

- Draw a rectangle with sides 16 cm × 12 cm.
- Calculate the area of the rectangle.
- Measure the diagonals of the rectangle.
- Mark the mid-points on all four sides.
- Connect the mid-points.

What shape do you have?

Can you easily calculate the area?

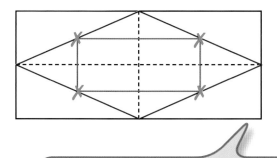

- Measure the diagonals of the second shape.
- Find and connect the mid-points of the second shape.

What shape do you have now?

What is the area of this shape?

1 Copy and complete this table of the properties of the shapes.

	Rectangle I	Rhombus I	Rectangle 2	Rhombus 2
Longest side (cm)	16	10	8	5
Shortest side (cm)	12	10	6	
Area (cm²)				
Diagonal I (cm)	20	16		8
Diagonal 2 (cm)	20		10	6

2 What patterns can you see?

3 Add two more columns to your table and use them to predict the measurements for the next rectangle and rhombus.

Continue to find and connect the mid-points and measure the diagonals until there is no more room.

4 Can you think of a way to calculate the areas of the rhombuses by cutting them out?

5 Using the information you have found here, think of a way to calculate the area of any rhombus.

  What patterns can you find if you start by drawing a square?

In the mirror

1 What is the mathematical name for each of these shapes?

2 What are the properties of each of these shapes?

3 Do they all have a line of symmetry?

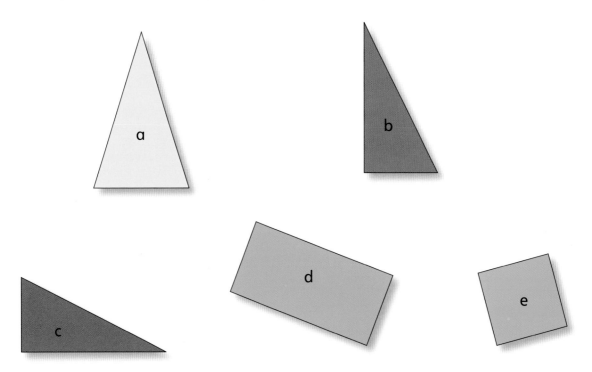

4 Which of the shapes fit together to make this shape?

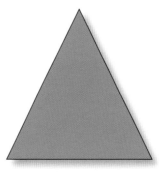

eXtra Work with a partner. Using a set of shapes from PCM 10 each make a symmetrical shape. Compare your shapes. Who has more lines of symmetry?

Polyominoes

Polyominoes are shapes made from identical squares that are placed together so that the squares share at least one side.

Shapes made with five identical squares are called pentominoes. The mathematician Solomon Golomb, who named pentominoes, labelled each different shape with the letter of the alphabet which it resembles.

These polyominoes are nets of an open cube.

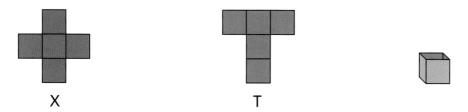

X   T

1   Draw these 10 pentominoes on squared paper and cut them out.

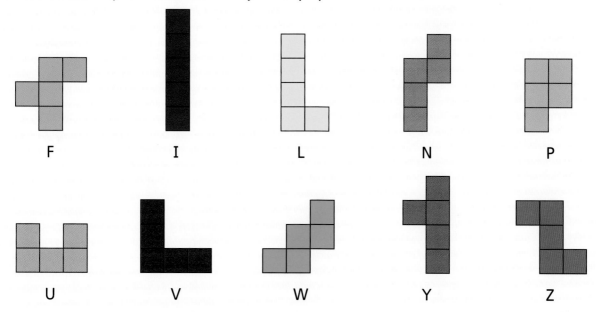

F   I   L   N   P

U   V   W   Y   Z

2   Which pentominoes fold into an open cube?

3   If each square is 1 cm², calculate the perimeters of the 12 pentominoes.

4   Which pentomino has the shortest perimeter? Which has the longest?
    Can you make up a rule for this?

eXtra

Hexominoes are polyominoes that are made with six identical squares. Can you find all 35 hexominoes? Predict which hexomino has the shortest perimeter. Predict which hexomino has the longest perimeter. Which of the hexominoes can be folded up into a closed cube?

Platonic solids

Why is a dice cube-shaped?

Plato

A famous mathematician and philosopher called Plato discovered that there were five solid shapes which could be made into fair dice. The five shapes are called Platonic solids. They each have particular properties which no other 3D shapes have.

The Platonic solids

| Cube | Tetrahedron | Octahedron | Icosahedron | Dodecahedron |

A **vertex** is the corner point of a polygon. The plural of vertex is **vertices**.

Measure the angles at each vertex of these shapes. What do you notice?

I Copy and complete this table of the five Platonic solids and their properties.

Shape	Number and shape of faces	Number of vertices	Number of edges	Size of each angle on each face
cube	6 square	8	12	90°
tetrahedron				
octahedron				
icosahedron				
dodecahedron				

These five solids are different to all other 3D shapes because, for each solid, all the faces are the same shape and size and all the angles are identical. They also have the same number of faces meeting at each vertex.

A cube dice is only fair if the arrangement of numbers on the faces is fair. Dice with I, 2, 3, 4, 5, 6 or 2, 2, 4, 4, 6, 6 are fair.

What if a dice had I, I, 2, 2, 4, 6 on the faces?

Use the internet to find out more about Plato and his Platonic solids. What can you find out about another mathematician called Euclid who proved Plato's work? Make the five Platonic solids and number the sides to use as dice. Are your dice fair?

Find the rule

Ali and Tom discuss ways that they could share £1. They make up a rule.

> If I give you 45p and I have 54p, there will be 1p left.

> I will keep 36p and you will have 63p. There will still be 1p left.

1 What is Tom and Ali's rule?
2 What other pairs of numbers will follow the same rule?
3 Will there always be 1p left over?

Tom thinks of a new rule.

> I will give you 26p and I will keep 62p. That leaves 12p.

> If I give you 71p and I keep 17p that will leave 12p too.

4 What other pairs of numbers follow this rule?

Tom and Ali then try 43p and 34p. This leaves them with 23p.

Which pairs of numbers will have:

5 34p left over?   6 45p left over?   7 56p left over?
8 What other amounts can be left over with this rule?

Sadie thinks about the rule.

> If I keep 82p, Ali will get 28p.

9 Explain to Sadie why that will not work.

10 Name three more pairs that would not work. Why don't they work?

What are the digit totals of each of these numbers: 56p and 65p, 47p and 74p? What other number pairs fit this rule? What are the digit totals of each of these numbers: 59p and 95p, 68p and 86p? What other number pairs fit this rule? Make up your own rule and find number pairs which follow it with other digit totals such as 12, 13 and 15.

Cross-numbers

				2
5				

Find the number below that matches each clue, then decide where the numbers go on the grid. Fill in your answers on PCM 12.

Some of the numbers fit onto the grid and some don't.

Some clues have more than one answer, so you will need to decide which one is best.

664	2896	8725	39	2996
366	29	6442	864	5499
74	169	44	5489	19

1 If I add this to 234, the total will be 600.

2 This number rounded to the nearest 1000 is 6000.

3 This number is 20 to the nearest 10.

4 Add 75 to this number to get to the nearest 100.

5 Add 4 to this number to get to the nearest 10.

6 This number is 100 to the nearest 100.

7 This number is 14 away from the nearest 50.

8 This number is 136 away from the nearest 1000.

9 This number rounded to the nearest 100 is 200.

10 This number is 0 to the nearest 100.

11 This number is 5500 to the nearest 10.

12 This number is 3000 to the nearest 10.

eXtra

Make up another cross-number using this grid, with numbers and clues of your own.

Doubling numbers

4 6 2 3

4000   600   20   3

To double 4623 we can double the thousands, the hundreds, the tens and the units and add them together.

$$8000 + 1200 + 40 + 6 = 9246$$

3 ·6 2

3   0·6   0·02

To double 3·62 we can double the units, tenths and hundredths and add them together.

$$6 + 1·2 + 0·04 = 7·24$$

Double these numbers.

1 324	2 271	3 476
4 562	5 776	6 3870
7 4207	8 5236	9 7826
10 6467	11 4·23	12 6·27
13 4·83	14 5·76	15 6·07

16 What is a good method to check your answers?

17 Check each of your answers using this method.

eXtra Use near doubles to find:
426 + 427   362 + 372   4671 + 4571   7·28 + 7·38

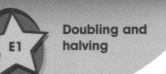
Half price sale

Do you like shopping in the sales?
What is the best bargain you have found?

Many clothes shops have sales at the end of each season. This is to get rid of old stock and make room for new stock. For example, shops want to sell all their leftover beach clothes at the end of the summer. This gives them room for all the winter clothes.

When shops are closing down they will also drop their prices. They will have a big sale so that they can sell everything and nothing goes to waste after the shop has closed.

Shops often have half price sales so that people can quickly work out what the new price of each item will be.

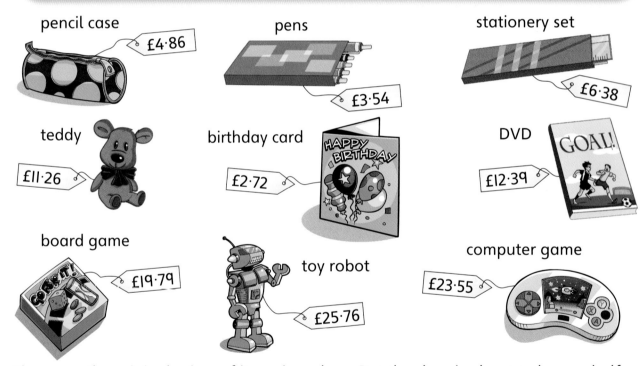

pencil case £4·86

pens £3·54

stationery set £6·38

teddy £11·26

birthday card £2·72

DVD £12·39

board game £19·79

toy robot £25·76

computer game £23·55

These are the original prices of items in a shop. But the shop is about to have a half price sale!

1 Draw up a table showing the original price and the sale price of each item.

2 You have £50. Use your table to see if you have enough to buy one of each of these items in the half price sale.

eXtra

You have £30 to spend on five different presents for five friends. What is the closest to £30 you can spend in the half price sale? How much is left over?

Improper fractions game

To change an improper fraction to a mixed number, divide the numerator by the denominator.

For example $\frac{17}{6} = 2 \text{ r } 5 = 2\frac{5}{6}$

Rules

- Each player should have a set of number cards 5–25, a dice and a copy of the number line on PCM 14.

- All shuffle your cards and each pick one at random. This will be the numerator of your fraction. Roll your dice. This will be the denominator.

- Now each work out where the fraction should go on your number line. For example if your card is 19 and the dice number is 6 your fraction will be $\frac{19}{6} = 3\frac{1}{3}$ and it should go between the 3 and the 4.

- If you get a numerator that is exactly divisible by the denominator and make a whole number then you miss your turn.

- Your aim is to have one fraction in each of the boxes above the number line. Whoever has a fraction in the most different boxes after 10 minutes is the winner.

After you have played the game, answer these questions.

1 Are some boxes easier to fill than others? Why?

2 What combinations produce a whole number?

3 What combinations of cards and dice are needed to make an improper fraction between 1 and 2?

4 What combinations of cards and dice are needed to make an improper fraction between 5 and 6?

5 What combinations of cards and dice are needed to make an improper fraction between 7 and 8?

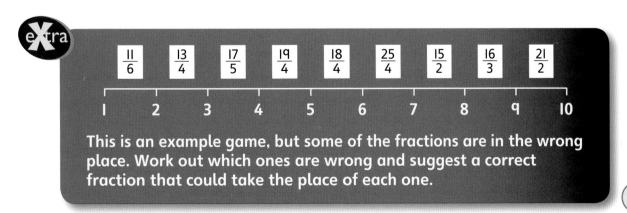

This is an example game, but some of the fractions are in the wrong place. Work out which ones are wrong and suggest a correct fraction that could take the place of each one.

Fractions

Reducing a fraction to its simplest form

Cancel the common factors in the numerator and denominator.
For example $\frac{42}{60}$.

Divide the numerator and the denominator by 2. $\frac{42}{60} = \frac{21}{30}$

Now divide the numerator and the denominator by 3. $\frac{21}{30} = \frac{7}{10}$

Write these fractions in their simplest forms.

1 $\frac{25}{40}$ 2 $\frac{28}{42}$ 3 $\frac{36}{60}$ 4 $\frac{45}{75}$ 5 $\frac{72}{90}$

Write these fractions in their simplest form and turn them into mixed numbers.

6 $\frac{20}{18}$ 7 $\frac{40}{24}$ 8 $\frac{50}{15}$ 9 $\frac{48}{20}$ 10 $\frac{39}{12}$

Comparing the size of two fractions

Rewrite both fractions with the common denominator then compare the fractions. For example which is larger, $\frac{3}{5}$ or $\frac{5}{8}$? Both denominators are factors of 40. Rewrite the fractions with 40 as the denominator.

$$\frac{3 \times 8 = 24}{5 \times 8 = 40} \qquad \frac{5 \times 5 = 25}{8 \times 5 = 40}$$

$\frac{25}{40}$ is greater than $\frac{24}{40}$ so we know that $\frac{5}{8}$ is greater than $\frac{3}{5}$.

Which is the larger fraction in each pair?

11 $\frac{4}{5}$ or $\frac{5}{7}$ 12 $\frac{2}{3}$ or $\frac{5}{8}$ 13 $\frac{5}{6}$ or $\frac{7}{9}$ 14 $\frac{1}{4}$ or $\frac{2}{7}$ 15 $\frac{9}{10}$ or $\frac{3}{4}$

 Using a common denominator, find the larger fraction of these pairs.

$\frac{3}{4}$ or $\frac{4}{5}$ $\frac{5}{6}$ or $\frac{6}{7}$ $\frac{6}{7}$ or $\frac{7}{8}$

What do you notice about the larger fraction in each pair?
Look at other similar pairs. Is this always the case?

Finding proportions

To make a chilli for eight people, Danny uses:

400 grams of beans

40 grams of tomato paste

4 onions

2 peppers

8 grams of chilli powder

16 tomatoes

320 grams of minced beef

1 Nasreen wants to use the same recipe, but she is only cooking for two people.

How much of each ingredient should she use?

2 Owen also uses this recipe, but he is cooking for 20 people.

How much of each ingredient should he use?

3 Petra uses the same recipe. She is cooking for five people.

How much of each ingredient should she use?

4 Roman uses the same recipe. He is cooking for 18 people.

How much of each ingredient should he use?

 Use the internet to find a recipe for your favourite dessert. Work out how much of each ingredient each of the children would need.

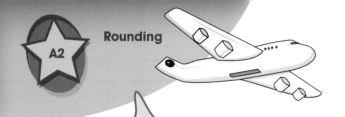

Rounding and converting distances

You are going on holiday to a secret destination. You know it is in Europe and it is 1000 km from London by air, to the nearest 1000 km.

Table 1 Distances from London in kilometres

Amsterdam	410 km	Lisbon	2240 km
Barcelona	1470 km	Marseilles	1250 km
Belgrade	2050 km	Milan	1290 km
Bern	960 km	Munich	1200 km
Bucharest	2590 km	Oslo	1670 km
Budapest	1700 km	Prague	1290 km
Copenhagen	1200 km	Sofia	2500 km
Düsseldorf	580 km	Stockholm	1820 km
Frankfurt	780 km	Venice	1590 km
Hamburg	850 km	Vienna	1500 km
Helsinki	2270 km	Warsaw	1590 km
Istanbul	3160 km	Zurich	950 km

1. Look at the distances from London to some major European cities in Table 1. Which cities could be your surprise destination?

2. Which city is 1800 km from London, rounded to the nearest 100 km?

3. Imagine you want to plan a trip to a city that is 2000 km from London rounded to the nearest 1000 km. Which cities could you choose from?

4. Which city is nearest to London and which city is furthest from London? How far are they from London? Give answers to the nearest 100 km.

5. A Boeing 747 aeroplane uses 50 gallons of fuel per 10 miles. Round each of the distances in Table 2 to the nearest 10 miles and calculate how much fuel the aeroplane will use for each journey.

6. The aeroplane will travel at approximately 500 mph. Divide each of the distances in the table by 500 to find approximately how long each journey will take. Give your answers to the nearest hour.

Table 2 Distances from London in miles

Athens, Greece	1486 miles
Beijing, China	5071 miles
Berlin, Germany	557 miles
Mumbai, India	4477 miles
Brussels, Belgium	199 miles
Cairo, Egypt	2187 miles
Jerusalem, Israel	2246 miles
Madrid, Spain	783 miles
Manila, Philippines	6679 miles
Moscow, Russia	1559 miles
Nairobi, Kenya	4228 miles
Sydney, Australia	10 562 miles

 eXtra

Wellington in New Zealand is 11 682 miles from London. Plan a trip to Wellington, stopping in one city from Table 1 or 2 on the way there and another on the way back. How long is the total journey in miles?

I mile is 1·609 km.

Imperial and metric conversions

For each item find out which amount is the greatest and which is the smallest. To compare each item you will need to convert the amounts into the same unit of measurement.

Record your answers in the table on PCM I5, using the suggested units of measurement given.

> I pint = 568 ml
> I pound = 454 grams
> I mile = 1·609 km

I   0·5 kg of cheese

    I lb of cheese

    450 g of cheese

5   A $\frac{1}{2}$ lb apple

    A 0·2 kg apple

    A 260 g apple

2   330 ml of milk

    $\frac{1}{2}$ pint of milk

    $\frac{1}{2}$ litre of milk

6   A rope I50 cm long

    A rope $\frac{1}{100}$ mile long

    A rope $\frac{1}{4}$ km long

3   A road 5 miles long

    A road 7·5 km long

    A road 750m long

7   A 5 kg rabbit

    A I0 lb rabbit

    A 4950g rabbit

4   500 ml of juice

    I pint of juice

    $\frac{3}{4}$ litre of juice

eXtra

Make a bag of pasta or rice of a certain weight, such as I kg or I lb. Make a piece of string of a certain length, such as I ft or I0 cm. Fill a plastic bottle with a certain amount of water, such as I pint or 330 ml.
Challenge other children in your class to estimate how heavy the bag is, how long the string is and how much water is in the bottle. Who is the closest?

Quick calculation without a calculator

The Trachtenberg System of Basic Mathematics is a method of doing high-speed multiplication, division, addition, subtraction and square roots without a calculator.

While a prisoner in the First World War, Jakow Trachtenberg devised a simple mental system for doing very difficult calculations. Later he escaped and perfected his system in Switzerland. He taught it to children who were doing badly at school. They loved it as, for the first time, they felt they were doing well in maths. In 1950, Trachtenberg founded the Mathematical Institute in Zurich.

The Trachtenberg method is fast and accurate and it is easy to double check answers. The Swiss still use the Trachtenberg method in all their banks!

The Trachtenberg method for multiplying by 11

Example: 1624 × 11

Step 1 The last digit of the **multiplicand** is the last digit of the answer.   **4**

> The **multiplicand** is the number being multiplied. In this case, the multiplicand is 1624.

Step 2 Add each of the digits of the multiplicand to the digit on its right.

2 + 4 = 6	**64**
6 + 2 = 8	**864**
1 + 6 = 7	**7864**

Step 3 The first digit of the multiplicand is the first digit of the answer.   **17 864**

Sometimes you will get a 2-digit number when you add a digit to its neighbour, for example 5 + 7 = 12. When this happens, write down the 2 and carry the 1 like you would for any addition. For example, 3571 × 11 = 39 281.

Use the Trachtenberg method to solve these calculations.

1 123 × 11	2 472 × 11	3 590 × 11	4 9203 × 11
5 7777 × 11	6 2835 × 11	7 12 321 × 11	8 40 404 × 11
9 80 808 × 11	10 243 × 110	11 5635 × 110	12 28 420 × 110

eXtra

Use the internet to explore Egyptian and Russian multiplication and try the following calculations using each of these methods. Show your working.
265 × 16   823 × 15   3167 × 73

Now try some calculations of your own using the methods you have learned about.

Investigating days and dates

Monday's child is fair of face,
Tuesday's child is full of grace,
Wednesday's child is full of woe,
Thursday's child has far to go,
Friday's child is loving and giving,
Saturday's child works hard for a living,
And the child that is born on the Sabbath day
Is bonny and wise, and good all day.

> Josh was born on a Sunday and his 21st birthday was on a Saturday. Josh was 21 in 2008. He was born in a summer month which had 30 days.

1 What could his date of birth have been?

2 On what day did Josh's 18th birthday fall?

3 What day were you born? Use a calendar to check.
   Work out the day on which your 21st birthday will fall.

4 Ask ten children in your class what day they were born.
   Predict the day on which each of their 21st birthdays will fall.

5 Ask if you can go to other classes in Year 3, Year 4 and Year 6 and collect the
   same information from a sample of ten children in each class.

Are the following statements always true, sometimes true or never true?

6 All children called Josh are born on a Sunday.

7 Children born on a Sunday have their 21st birthday on a Saturday.

8 Children born on a Sunday in the same year will all have their 21st birthday on the
   same day of the week.

9 How many days will you have been alive for on your 21st birthday? You should
   include the day you were born and the day of your 21st birthday.

10 Will everyone else have been alive for the same number of days as you on their
   21st birthday?

eXtra

**Why do we have leap years? Who decided we needed them?
Use reference books or the internet to find out.
When do you think people who were born on a leap day
(February 29th) celebrate their birthday? Do you know
anyone born on a leap day? If so, what do they do?**

Common multiples and prime factors

60	24	25	84
36	15	9	30
12	21	40	42
20	18	14	35

1 From the grid, choose one set of three numbers that are common multiples and say what they are multiples of.

> For example 60, 40 and 20 are multiples of 2, 4, 5, 10 and 20

2 Find five other sets of three numbers which are common multiples and say what they are common multiples of.

3 Can you find a set of four common multiples in the table?

4 Can you find a set of five common multiples in the table?

5 Can you find a set of six common multiples in the table?

Look at these factor trees.

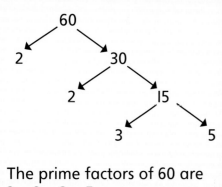

The prime factors of 60 are
$2 \times 2 \times 3 \times 5$

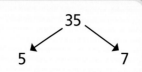

The prime factors of 35 are 5×7

6 For each of the numbers in the table above, find the prime factors using a factor tree.

7 What do you notice about all the numbers at the ends of the lines?

eXtra Look at your sets of three common multiples from question 2. Compare their prime factors. What do you notice?

Multiplication investigation

1 Copy and complete this multiplication grid:

×	200	70	6
30			
2			

2 How does this grid help you to solve the problem 276 × 32?

3 Predict which of these five questions has the largest answer.
Predict which has the smallest answer.

   a 438 × 27   **b** 452 × 35   **c** 36 × 291

   d 45 × 383   **e** 306 × 67

4 Draw grids like the one above to solve these problems and check your predictions.

For each pair of multiplications, use grids to help you investigate which will give the larger product.

5 444 × 55 or 555 × 44

6 333 × 77 or 777 × 33

7 999 × 22 or 222 × 99

8 How can you explain what you have found?

Now try drawing grids to solve calculations multiplying 3-digit numbers together.

For each pair, investigate which will give the larger product and why.

272 × 727 or 772 × 227   722 × 277 or 777 × 222

Egyptian multiplication

The Ancient Egyptians used symbols to represent numbers:

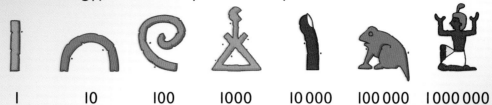

| 1 | 10 | 100 | 1000 | 10 000 | 100 000 | 1 000 000 |

There was no symbol for zero.
They had to draw several of each symbol for each number.

For example, 213 would be written as

Have a go at writing some other numbers using the Ancient Egyptian symbols.

The Egyptians had their own way of solving multiplications. They used doubling.

To solve 46 × 23, draw a table with 1 in the left-hand column and 23 in the right-hand column. Double the numbers in each column until the number in the left-hand column is greater than 46.

1	23
2	46
4	92
8	184
16	368
32	736
64	1472

Find the numbers in the left-hand column that total 46.

32 + 8 + 4 + 2 = 46

Add together the corresponding numbers in the right-hand column.

736 + 184 + 92 + 46 = 1058

Check your answer using another method or with a calculator.

Estimate the answers to the following calculations, then use the Egyptian method to find the answers.

1 21 × 36 **2** 31 × 27 **3** 39 × 52 **4** 53 × 28 **5** 77 × 43

eXtra Does this method work with 3-digit numbers? Make up some calculations with 3-digit numbers and try it out!

Double up!

> Would you rather have £1000 now, or start with £20 and double it each day for a week?

> I have £20 on Monday. How much will I have by Sunday?
> Monday – £20, Tuesday – £40, Wednesday – £80, Thursday – £160, Friday – £320, Saturday – £640, Sunday – £1280
>
> I end up with £1280 so I think I would rather double £20 each day than have £1000 now!

Would you rather have:

1 £2000 now or start with £3 and double it every day for 10 days?

2 £100 000 now or start with £7 and double it every day for 15 days?

3 £1 000 000 now or start with £5 and double it every day for 20 days?

> How have you recorded your doubling?
> Do you have a system?
> Do you think this is the best way?

You start with £1. Predict how many times you will need to double your money to reach each amount below. Find the answers and compare them to your predictions. How close were you?

4 £1000

5 £10 000

6 £100 000

7 £1 000 000

 Look at the questions 4–7 again but this time try tripling the numbers instead of doubling them. What do you find?

Coordinates

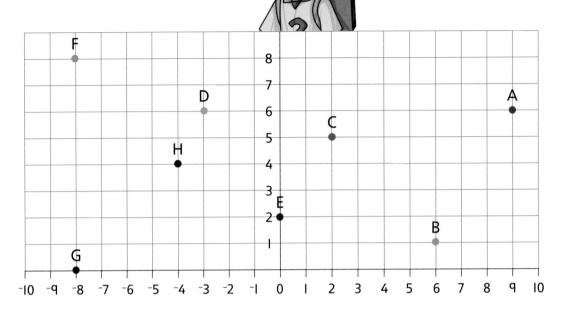

I   What are the coordinates of points A to H?

Look at PCM 17. Follow the instruction for each shape and copy it carefully to its new position. Give the coordinates for the corners of each shape at its new position.

2   Shape A slides 8 squares to the left.

3   Shape B slides 10 squares to the left and 2 squares up.

4   Shape C slides 6 squares to the right and 4 squares down.

5   Shape D slides 8 squares to the right and 3 squares up.

6   Shape E slides 8 squares to the left and 7 squares down. Give the coordinates for the corners of the shape, without drawing it.

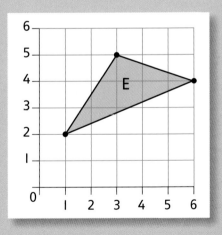

eXtra   Use the blank grids on PCM 18 to make up some puzzles like these for other children in the group. You will need to write the questions and prepare an answer sheet! If you draw a very large shape on the grid how far can you slide it? What if you draw a very small shape?

Investigating diagonals

How many diagonals does each of these pentagons have?

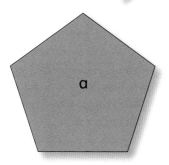

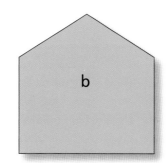

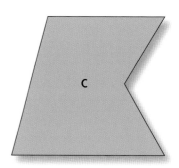

1 For each pentagon, draw each diagonal on a blank shape on PCM 20.

2 How many diagonals does each pentagon have? Does each pentagon have the same number of diagonals?

Taking each pentagon in turn, look at the two shapes made by each diagonal. For example this diagonal cuts the pentagon into an isosceles triangle and a rectangle.

3 What two shapes does each diagonal produce? Is this different for each of the different pentagons?

Now do the same with these hexagons.

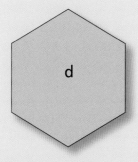

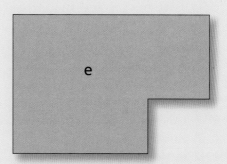

4 How many diagonals does each shape have? What shapes does each diagonal make?

5 Draw a different hexagon and investigate the shapes made by its diagonals.

Investigate the diagonals of octagons. Can you predict what different shapes will be formed?

37

Stamp sizes

The Royal Mail makes postage stamps of different sizes and different values.

You can have your own design printed onto stamps and order a sheet of them.

Stamps come in four different sizes and are printed on A4, A3, A2, A1 or A0 size sheets of paper.

Table 1 Stamp sizes in mm

	Width	Height	Area
a	34·7 mm	36·5 mm	mm²
b	20·3 mm	24·1 mm	mm²
c	41 mm	26 mm	mm²
d	40·6 mm	29·8 mm	mm²

Table 2 Paper sizes in mm

	Width	Height	Area
A4	210 mm	297 mm	mm²
A3	297 mm	420 mm	mm²
A2	420 mm	594 mm	mm²
A1	594 mm	841 mm	mm²
A0	841 mm	1189 mm	mm²

1 Copy and complete Table 1 to find the area of each stamp.

> An A0 size piece of paper has an area of approximately 1 m².

2 Copy and complete Table 2 to find the area of each sheet of paper.

> If I want stamp b on A4 paper, I can fit the stamps in two different ways.
> If the stamps are arranged in portrait I could get 120 stamps per sheet.
> If the stamps are arranged in landscape I can get 112 stamps per sheet.

10 stamps across

12 stamps down

Portrait

14 stamps across

8 stamps down

Landscape

3 Explore how many of stamp b can be cut from the other sized sheets of paper. Think about how much paper is wasted each time.

4 Which paper size and layout is the most efficient? Why?

eXtra   The most common stamps cost 27p, 36p, 50p or 56p per stamp. The stamps are the same size as stamp **a** in Table 1. At each price what is the value of an A4 sheet, for stamp size, portrait and landscape?

Area and perimeter

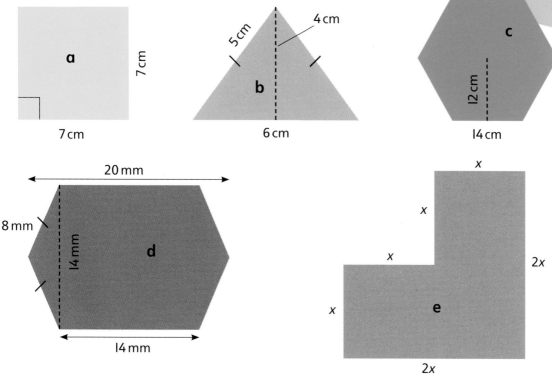

Which shape matches each statement?

If a statement does not match a shape, explain why the statement is wrong.

1 The perimeter of this shape is 6 × 14 cm.

2 The area of this shape is 4 × 7 cm.

3 The perimeter of this shape is 8x.

4 The area of this shape is 49 cm².

5 The perimeter of this shape is 6 cm + 5 cm + 5 cm.

6 The area of this shape is 6 × 14 cm.

7 The perimeter of this shape is 2 (14 + 8 + 8) mm.

8 The areas of these shapes cannot be calculated because they are irregular.

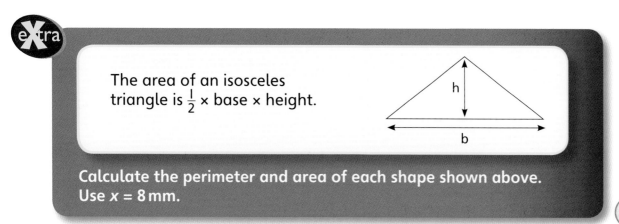

eXtra

The area of an isosceles triangle is $\frac{1}{2}$ × base × height.

Calculate the perimeter and area of each shape shown above.
Use x = 8 mm.

Calendars

Pope Gregory XIII

The Gregorian calendar was devised by Pope Gregory XIII in 1582 and was used throughout Europe. It was not introduced into Great Britain until 1752. Today it is used throughout the world.

The Gregorian calendar replaced the Julian calendar which was introduced by Julius Caesar, the Roman leader, in about 45 BC. The Julian calendar was found to be inaccurate in the calculation of leap years. The Gregorian calendar improved this by dropping three leap days every 400 years, but there is still a slight inaccuracy of 1 day per 3000 years.

Julius Caesar

The Gregorian calendar has a 146 097 day cycle, exactly 20 871 weeks or 400 years. So, for example, the days of the week in the Gregorian calendar in 1603 were exactly the same as for 2003. This means more months begin on a Sunday than any other day of the week and therefore have a Friday 13th.

The month names and number of days in each month come from the Romans. It is said that July and August both have 31 days because Julius Caesar's heir, Caesar Augustus, wanted his month to have as many days as Julius Caesar's!

1   Use the internet to find out as much as you can about the Julian and Gregorian calendars. Think about the similarities and differences.

An average year is 365·2425 days.

2   How many weeks is an average year?

3   How many hours?

4   How many minutes?

5   How many seconds?

6   If a non-leap year is 365 days and a leap-year is 366 days, how many more seconds are there in a leap year than in a non-leap year?

7   Some think our time system should be decimal with 100 hours in a day and 100 minutes in an hour. Is this a good idea? Explain your decision.

All world time is given by the Atomic Clock. It has been used since 1955 and is adjusted every three minutes.

8   Use the internet to find out as much as you can about the Atomic Clock.

eXtra

Omar Khayyam also devised a calendar. Use the internet to research his calendar. Compare it to the Gregorian calendar and the Julian calendar. Which do you think is the most accurate? Explain why.

Number patterns

Anya, Bilal, Cassie, David, Elsa and Freddie all live in the same village.

The village is five miles from school and there is no school bus so they are each taken to school in the car by one of their relatives.

The six families decide to save petrol and work out a rota to share the drive to school. Each driver can take all six children to school.

But

Anya's grandma can only drive every two days, beginning on day 2.

Bilal's dad can only drive every three days, beginning on day 3.

Cassie's mum can drive every five days, beginning any day.

David's dad can drive every six days, beginning any day.

Elsa's mum can drive every 10 days, beginning any day.

Freddie's uncle can drive every 15 days, beginning any day.

> There are 30 school days each term and there are five school days in a week. Don't count weekends.

> Can the children get to school every day for a term?

1 Find out if this is possible. Explain how you have investigated this and what you have found out.

2 Work out a fair rota to share the days out evenly.

 Two of the drivers are willing to change their day and how often they drive. Suggest who it should be. Explain why you have chosen these two people.

Schedules

You are the controller of a television channel for the day. Choose from the programmes below to create the schedule for next week's television, from Monday to Friday. Remember that there are some rules you need to follow.

- Programmes begin at 16:00 and finish at 17:59 so you have a time slot of 1 hour and 59 minutes each day.
- Each day's schedule must include one animal programme, one news programme, one competition and one sports programme.
- A programme cannot be on twice in one week.
- Leave one minute between each programme for adverts.
- A news programme is never on last, but on a Friday it must be on after 17:30.
- An animal programme is never on first.

Complete the schedule on PCM 22. Give all times using the 24-hour clock.

Animal programmes
Looking After Dogs	12 minutes
Snakes!	28 minutes
Our Clever Pets	28 minutes
African Safari	29 minutes
Amazing Animals	53 minutes

News programmes
Pop News	29 minutes
World News	9 minutes
Local News	10 minutes
Film News	29 minutes
News Round-up	9 minutes

Competitions
The Music Quiz	13 minutes
Painting Contest	4 minutes
Race the Clock	30 minutes
Guess the Celebrity	9 minutes
Can You Spell?	30 minutes

Sports programmes
Ladies' Triathlon	48 minutes
Football Highlights	75 minutes
Cycling	45 minutes
Swimming for Gold	45 minutes
Hockey Tips	45 minutes

 e**X**tra

Find the total time that each category of programme is on for each week. Would you change the allocation for any of the categories and why?

The time slot for each day has been increased by 30 minutes.

How would you share this extra time between the four categories? Explain your decision.

Perfect numbers

Nobody knows exactly when perfect numbers were discovered but it is thought that the Ancient Egyptians may have known about them. The famous mathematician Pythagoras studied them and believed they had mystical properties.

A perfect number is found by adding together the factors of the number (not including the number itself). If the sum of the factors is the same as the number we started with then it is a perfect number.

Pythagoras

1 Copy and complete this table to work out which of these are perfect numbers. Remember not to include the number itself when finding the sum of the factors.

Number	Factors	Sum of factors
1	1	0
2	1, 2	1
3	1, 3	1
4	1, 2, 4	
5	1, 5	
6	1, 2, 3, 6	
7		
8		
9		
10		
11		
12		

Mathematicians have been searching for perfect numbers for hundreds of years. They have only discovered 46. The largest known perfect number was discovered in 2008 and has more than 12 000 000 digits. There may still be other perfect numbers smaller than this, that are yet to be found. Mathematicians think that all perfect numbers end in 6 or 8, are always even and are also triangular numbers.

2 Continue the table above to find the next perfect number.

Use the internet to find out more about perfect numbers. How many perfect numbers can you find? What are they? Who discovered them? When?

Adding with a difference

1	2	3	4
5	6	7	8
9	10	11	12
13	14	15	16

1. Find the totals of the two numbers in diagonally opposite corners. Add the pairs.

2. What do you notice about where these number pairs are on the grid?

3. Using these properties, what other pairs of number pairs can you find that add up to 34?

4. Find the totals of the two numbers in diagonally opposite corners. What is the total of all four numbers?

5. What other pairs of numbers can you find that have this total?

7	8	9	10	11	12
15	16	17	18	19	20
23	24	25	26	27	28
31	32	33	34	35	36
39	40	41	42	43	44
47	48	49	50	51	52

1	2	3	4	5
6	7	8	9	10
11	12	13	14	15
16	17	18	19	20
21	22	23	24	25

6. Does this table have the same properties?

7. Use the properties that you have noticed to find out the missing corner number.

8. Find the totals of the two numbers in diagonally opposite corners. What is the total of all four numbers?

9. Use the properties of the grid to fill in the missing numbers.

1			7
	11	13	
	19		23
25			

eXtra

Make your own 7 × 7 square that follows this rule.
Make an 8 × 8 square that follows this rule.
Can you make an even bigger square than that?

Fair share

You and your friend have 20 boxes of chocolates between you.

Each box contains a different number of chocolates. The first box has I chocolate, the second box has 2, the third has 3, … and so on up to the 20th box which has 20 chocolates.

Box I **Box 2** **Box 3** **Box 4**

You and your friend must share the boxes between you so that you each have the same number of chocolates.

But: you are not going to share them all out at once! You are going to work out which sets of consecutive boxes you can share out equally.

Each set must include box I.

Example: boxes I, 2 and 3

Example: boxes I, 2, 3 and 4

I   Is it possible to have four chocolates each? How do you know?

> I cannot share out boxes I to 5 equally, or boxes I to 6.
> But I can share out boxes I to 7.

2   What other sets of consecutive boxes can you share out fairly?

 What if you had to use the same rules to share sets of consecutive boxes between you and two friends?

Odd one out

For each question one answer is not correct. Find the two correct answers, then find the odd one out and say why it is wrong.

Use inverses and your calculator to find the answers.
You can try other ways of checking if you think of any.

1 I am a whole number. This is the answer when I am multiplied by 6.

    a 456   **b** 645   **c** 546

2 I am a whole number. This is the answer when I am multiplied by 0·66.

    a 1518   **b** 330   **c** 752

3 I am a positive number. This is the answer when 763 is added to me.

    a 4726   **b** 1998   **c** 263

4 I am the weight of a bag of rice in whole grams. This is the total weight of 14 identical bags of rice.

    a 6320 g   **b** 11 928 g   **c** 17 402 g

5 I am a decimal number. This is the answer when I am halved and 365 is added.

    a 401·05   **b** 1095   **c** 865·7

6 I am a multiple of 2. This is the answer when I am multiplied by 3 and 175 is added.

    a 1453   **b** 520   **c** 421

Some ants have a relay race on a track which is 80 m long.

Each ant runs exactly the same distance.

Find out how far each ant runs in whole mm if there are:

    a 400 ants   **b** 500 ants   **c** 300 ants

The ants decide to make a line, heads touching tails. Each ant is 6 mm long. How long would each of the possible teams stretch in metres?

Money steps

Get across the swamp in six steps. You can go forwards,
or diagonally but not back. When you step on a stone you collect
that money. But when you step on a crocodile it will snatch money away from you!
Note how much money you have at each step. You cannot step on a crocodile unless
you have enough money for it to take.

Start

£17·89   £3·45   £0·99   £5·15

£2·56   5p   £3·00   £2·32

£14·69   £4·40   £15·05   £1·05

£1·01   £2·50   £0·92   £40·01

174p   £0·75   22p   £60

Finish

1 What is the largest amount of money you can collect in six steps?

2 What is the smallest amount of money you can collect without losing it all?

**How many different ways are there to cross the swamp
in six steps? Try using counters to mark the routes.
Do any routes make you lose all your money?**

47

Multiplication problems with time

Which is longer, 52 days or 1250 hours?

There are 24 hours in a day, so multiply 52 by 24 to compare.

$$
\begin{array}{r}
5\ 2 \\
\times\quad 2\ 4 \\
\hline
2\ 0\ 8 \\
\hline
1\ 0\ 4\ 0 \\
\hline
=\ 1\ 2\ 4\ 8 \\
\end{array}
$$

$52 \times 24 = 1248$ so 1250 hours is 2 hours longer than 52 days.

Which time is longer and by how much?

First estimate, then use the method above to find the answer.

1 40 days or 900 hours?

2 84 days or 2000 hours?

3 100 days or 2500 hours?

4 123 days or 3000 hours?

5 154 weeks or 1000 days?

6 262 weeks or 2000 days?

7 678 weeks or 5000 days?

8 24 hours or 1500 minutes?

9 86 hours or 5000 minutes?

10 7 days or 10 000 minutes?

Make up some more problems like this, involving days and years. Remember every fourth year is a leap year!

Decimal multiplication

When multiplying with decimals it is useful to estimate your answer first to help you check your answer.

I know that 15·3 × 6 is around 90.

```
    1 5 · 3
  ×   6
  ─────────
      1 · 8
    3 0
    6 0
  ─────────
  = 9 1 · 8
  ─────────
```

I know that 4·72 × 7 is around 30.

```
      4 · 7 2
  ×     7
  ───────────
      0 · 1 4
      4 · 9
    2 8
  ───────────
  = 3 3 · 0 4
  ───────────
        1   1
```

Try these examples. Remember to set out your working carefully.

Don't forget to estimate first!

1 23·2 × 4
2 43·6 × 8
3 5·36 × 3
4 7·67 × 6
5 32·8 × 5
6 70·9 × 7
7 3·07 × 9
8 65·3 × 6

These are the prices of some items in a stationery shop.

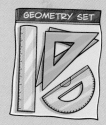

£6·35

£1·79

£3·96

£8·05

Find the cost of:

9 seven pens
10 six geometry sets
11 four exercise books
12 nine rulers

Arrange the digits 6, 3, 7 and 9 to make a multiplication in the format TU·t × U.
Which arrangement of digits gives the largest product?
Which gives the smallest product?
What if the 6 were replaced with a 1?

Fractional amounts

After finding a fraction of a number, Hassan was left with 24.

The fraction question could have been $\frac{1}{2}$ of 48 = 24.

It could have been $\frac{2}{3}$ of 36 = 24.

I Give five more fraction questions that have the answer 24.

When Gabrielle found a fraction of a number, she was left with 20.

2 What might Gabrielle's fraction question have been? Give five suggestions.

Fractions game

- Take turns to think of a fraction of a number that gives one of the numbers on the game board.

- Check your answer with your opponent.

- Cover your number with a counter.

- Where a number is on the grid more than once, a different fraction must be used each time.

- The winner is the first person to get a line of four counters horizontally, vertically or diagonally.

10	12	50	12	12
25	40	30	48	30
16	48	16	25	10
25	30	40	40	16
27	10	12	50	27

eXtra Play again, but this time don't use any unit fractions.

A unit fraction has a numerator of I. For example $\frac{1}{4}$.

Fractions problems

A paradox is a statement that seems to contradict itself, but may be true.

The Greek Philosopher Zeno was very interested in logic puzzles. He devised a set of problems to challenge what we believe about the world.

The paradox of Achilles and the tortoise
Achilles arranges a 1000 metre race with a tortoise.
They start running at the same time but Achilles gives the tortoise a head start of 200 metres. Achilles runs at 200 metres a minute. The tortoise runs at 10 metres a minute.
After one minute Achilles will have run 200 metres, and will get to the tortoise's starting point. During this time, the tortoise will run 10 metres.
It will then take Achilles some time to run the next 10 metres and during this time the tortoise will have moved further on.
It will take more time again for Achilles to reach this third point, and the tortoise will keep moving ahead.

Therefore whenever Achilles reaches somewhere that the tortoise has been, he still has further to go. Achilles can never overtake the tortoise!

Which is the longer distance:

1 $\frac{3}{4}$ of the track or $\frac{7}{10}$ of the track?   2 $\frac{5}{8}$ or $\frac{3}{5}$ of the track?

3 $\frac{7}{20}$ or $\frac{9}{25}$ of the track?   4 $\frac{33}{40}$ or $\frac{7}{8}$ of the track?   5 $\frac{13}{50}$ or $\frac{1}{4}$ of the track?

How long does Achilles take to travel:

6 $\frac{4}{5}$ of the course?   7 $\frac{3}{10}$ of the course?   8 $\frac{16}{25}$ of the course?

How long does the tortoise take to travel:

9 $\frac{9}{20}$ of the course?   10 $\frac{3}{4}$ of the course?   11 $\frac{27}{40}$ of the course?

12 Who do you think will win the race?
Try to explain why the story of Achilles and the tortoise is a paradox.

 e**X**tra If the race was 1600 metres, how long would it take Achilles to travel the distances in questions 6–8? How long would it take the tortoise to travel the distances in questions 9–11?

Divisibility

Here are two methods for finding out if 3-digit numbers are divisible by 7.

Method I
Double the hundreds digit and add this to the remaining part of the number. If the total is divisible by 7, then so is the number.

Method 2
Double the last digit of the number and subtract this from the remaining digits. If the total is divisible by 7, then so is the number.

For example, 539.

| **Method I** | $5 \times 2 = 10$ | $10 + 39 = 49$ | 49 is divisible by 7 |
| **Method 2** | $9 \times 2 = 18$ | $53 - 18 = 35$ | 35 is divisible by 7 |

$$539 \div 7 = 77 \qquad 539 \text{ is divisible by 7!}$$

Use either method to check if the following numbers are divisible by 7.

1 (175) 2 (276) 3 (322) 4 (987) 5 (455)

6 (531) 7 (368) 8 (815) 9 (906) 10 (644)

Method I can also be used for 4-digit numbers.

Double the first two digits as if they were a 2-digit number. Add this to the remaining part of the number. If the total is divisible by 7, then so is the number.

For example, 2387.

$$23 \times 2 = 46 \qquad 46 + 87 = 133 \qquad 33 \text{ is divisible by 7}$$

$$2387 \div 7 = 341 \qquad 2387 \text{ is divisible by 7!}$$

II Use this method to find five more 4-digit numbers that are divisible by 7. Show your working.

eXtra

Remind yourself of the rules for finding if numbers are divisible by 3. Use any combination of the methods you have learned to find six 3- or 4-digit numbers that are divisible by both 3 and 7. Divide these numbers by 21. What do you notice? Why is this?

Extreme temperatures

Gabriel Daniel Fahrenheit

Do you listen to the weather forecast?

In Europe temperatures are given in Celsius. In the USA Fahrenheit is used. Fahrenheit and Celsius were named after scientists, Gabriel Daniel Fahrenheit and Anders Celsius.

Anders Celsius

Table 1 The top ten coldest inhabited cities in the world

Country	City	Average temperature
Antarctica	Plateau Station	⁻119·2 degrees Fahrenheit
Antarctica	Vostok	⁻128·6 degrees Fahrenheit
Canada	Fort Selkirk	⁻86·8 degrees Fahrenheit
Canada	Snag	⁻96·0 degrees Fahrenheit
Greenland	Eismitte	⁻84·8 degrees Fahrenheit
Greenland	Northice	⁻74·0 degrees Fahrenheit
Russia	Oymyakon	⁻81·4 degrees Fahrenheit
Russia	Verkhoyansk	⁻89·8 degrees Fahrenheit
USA	Prospect Creek	⁻79·8 degrees Fahrenheit
USA	Rogers Pass	⁻69·7 degrees Fahrenheit

1 Write the cities in Table 1 in order from the coldest to the least cold.

Table 2 The top ten hottest inhabited cities in the world

Country	City	Average temperature
Mali	Timbuktu	83·5 degrees Fahrenheit
Niger	Niamey	84·0 degrees Fahrenheit
Republic of Yemen	Aden	83·9 degrees Fahrenheit
Sudan	Khartoum	84·6 degrees Fahrenheit
Sudan	Omdurman	84·6 degrees Fahrenheit
Tamil Nadu, India	Madras	84·7 degrees Fahrenheit
Tamil Nadu, India	Madurai	84·0 degrees Fahrenheit
Tamil Nadu, India	Tiruchirapalli	83·8 degrees Fahrenheit
Tamil Nadu, India	Tirunelveli	84·7 degrees Fahrenheit
Burkina Faso	Ouagadougou	83·5 degrees Fahrenheit

2 Write the cities in Table 2 in order from the hottest to the least hot.

3 Choose one city from each table. Calculate the difference in temperature if you travelled from one city to the other.

e**X**tra Do you prefer to use Celsius or Fahrenheit for temperature? Why? Can you find out how to convert from Fahrenheit to Celsius?

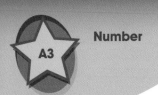

Using your calculator

Imagine you can only use these buttons on your calculator:

What calculations can you use to make each number between ⁻10 and 20?

1 Copy and complete this table to show how you can make each number. The first one has been done for you.

Number	Calculation	Number	Calculation	Number	Calculation
⁻10	5 − 5 − 5 − 5 =	1		11	
⁻9		2		12	
⁻8		3		13	
⁻7		4		14	
⁻6		5		15	
⁻5		6		16	
⁻4		7		17	
⁻3		8		18	
⁻2		9		19	
⁻1		10		20	

Now imagine you can only use these buttons on your calculator:

2 Copy and complete this table to show how you can make each of these numbers.

Number	Calculation
60	
59	
63	
80	
1480	

 I dropped my calculator and broke the 1 key.

Help me make each of these numbers without using 1.
Is there more than one way to make each number?

101   210   5161

Working with seconds

Table I Qualifying times for a swimming championship

		Aged 9	Aged 10	Aged II	Aged 12
50 m Freestyle	Boys	39·00	35·50	33·00	32·00
	Girls	39·00	35·50	33·00	32·00
50 m Backstroke	Boys	45·00	42·00	39·50	38·00
	Girls	45·00	41·50	40·00	38·00

I Complete the first table on PCM 26 to find out who qualified for the championship.

Table 2 Winners' times from the 200 m sprint race on Sports Day

Name	Position	Time in seconds
Kadi	Ist	24·87
Nadine	2nd	
Zahra	3rd	25·89

2 What could Nadine's time have been, to the nearest hundredth of a second?

3 How many seconds faster was Kadi than Zahra?

The wind slowed each of the runners down by 0·9 seconds.

4 If there had been no wind what would Kadi's and Zahra's finishing times have been?

5 What would Nadine's fastest possible time have been, to two decimal places, if there had been no wind?

Table 3 2008 Beijing Olympics Men's Cycling Sprint Quarterfinal times

Name	Time
HOY Chris (GB)	10·636
SIREAU Kevin (FR)	10·570
KENNY Jason (GB)	10·531
AWANG Mohd Azizulhasni (MA)	11·010
MULDER Teun (NE)	10·888
BOS Theo (NE)	10·777
BOURGAIN Mickael (FR)	10·734
LEVY Maximilian (DE)	10·763

6 Complete the table on PCM 26 by writing each time to the nearest tenth of a second and deciding the position in which each cyclist finished the race.

 e**X**tra Find out who won the Cycling Men's Sprint finals at the 2008 Olympics in Beijing. How much faster was he in Race 2 than in Race I?

A different way to multiply

Use the Vedic method to work out how much these sheets of stamps will cost.

1

2

3

4

5

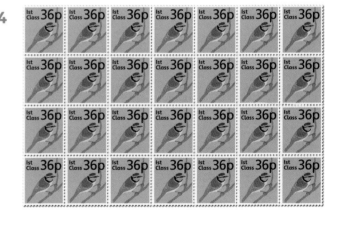

e**X**tra

Can you use this method for any 2-digit numbers? Make up some 2-digit multiplications of your own and try them out using the Vedic method.

Find out more about Vedic Mathematics on the internet.

Solving money matters

The head teacher has been thinking about where to go for the school camping trip this year.

She has contacted three camp sites but needs help deciding which one to choose.

Trip details
Monday 22nd June to Friday 26th June (four nights).
124 children (half boys, half girls) and six adults (four females and two males) will be going on the trip. Females and males must be accommodated in separate tents. Adults and children must be accommodated in separate tents.

	Activities	Cost per person per night	Cost per tent	Cost for three meals per day	Cost of transport
Sunny Vale Camp Site	• Swimming • Sailing • Rock climbing • Walking	£3·50 (Discount of 10% for 4 nights or more)	• To sleep 6 £10·00 per night • To sleep 4 £7.00 per night	£6·00 per person	• Coaches for 40 people £600 per week • Coaches for 45 people £650 per week
Happy Days Camp Site	• Swimming • Woodcraft • Go karting • Walking	£3·25	• To sleep 8 £12·00 per night • To sleep 2 £3·00 per night	£ 6·50 per person	• Coaches for 50 people £700 per week • Coaches for 20 people £400 per week
Wonder Hills Camp Site	• Swimming • Bungee jumping • Cycling • Walking	Free	• To sleep 10 £100 per week • To sleep 2 £50 per week	£3 per meal per person (Half price for children)	• Coaches for 35 people £400 per week • Coaches for 20 people £200 per week

Calculate which venue will be the most cost effective.

1 How many coaches are needed for transport to each camp and for trips?

2 What size of tents will you hire? How many will you need?

3 Which camp site works out the cheapest overall?

4 How much will you charge each child for the trip?

5 Which campsite would you choose? Why?

Compare your choice with other children in the class and together decide on one venue. Think about which activities will be most popular.

 eXtra

Write a report for the head teacher showing your calculations and giving reasons for your choice of camp site.

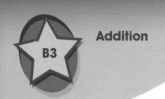

Big addition game

- **Player 1:** choose two numbers from the grid to make a total for question 1. Choose a method of addition and record your workings. Try to find another solution for question 1, using different numbers.

- **Player 2:** try to find two more ways to make a total for question 1.

- Check each other's solutions.

- Score one point for each correct answer.

- Repeat for questions 2–9. Take turns to be the first player to answer a question.

5623	4039	1073	2288
3402	2198	4329	6924
7810	8007	6291	7201
5209	4092	5411	4236

1 Add two numbers so that you have a zero in the units place.

2 Add two numbers so that you have a zero in the tens place.

3 Add two numbers so that you have a zero in the hundreds place.

4 Add two numbers so that the total is more than ten thousand.

5 Add two numbers so that the total is less than six thousand.

6 Add two numbers so that the total is between six and eight thousand.

7 Add two numbers so that the total is between eleven and twelve thousand.

8 Add three numbers so that the total is more than fifteen thousand.

9 Add three numbers so that the total is less than seven thousand.

If you have a tie break:
Who is the first to find two pairs of numbers that have the same total?

eXtra Using the same number grid, make up some more questions like these to challenge your friends.

Decimal spin off

Rules

- Play with a partner. Each choose a different colour of counters.
- Take turns to spin the spinner on PCM 30 twice.
- Add the two numbers using column addition. Show your workings.
- Cover the answer on the grid with one of your counters.
- The winner is the first player to get three counters in a row, horizontally, vertically or diagonally.
- If your answer has already been taken by your opponent, miss a go.

6·1	0·86	0·12	1·6	12·08	10·4
28·14	22·9	22·16	44·2	6·84	1·14
6·067	0·827	0·087	22·127	0·054	5·77
13·246	8·006	7·266	29·306	7·233	14·412
6·61	1·37	0·63	22·67	0·597	7·776
11·24	6	5·26	27·3	5·227	12·406

eXtra Play again but this time spin the spinner three times and choose which two numbers you want to use for your answer. Try blocking your opponent!

Heavy reading

William, Caitlin and Salim found the eight heaviest books in the school library.
Their weights were:

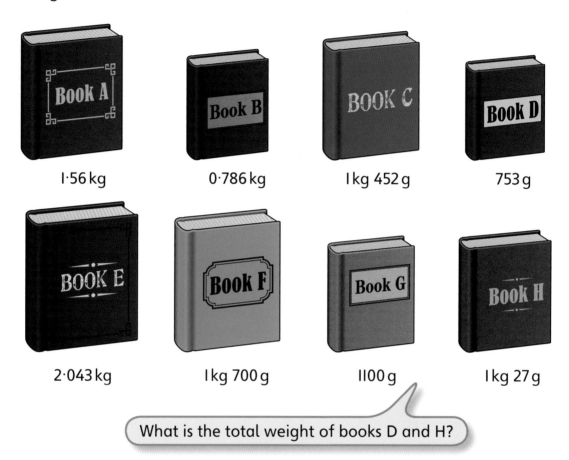

Book A — 1·56 kg

Book B — 0·786 kg

BOOK C — 1 kg 452 g

Book D — 753 g

BOOK E — 2·043 kg

Book F — 1 kg 700 g

Book G — 1100 g

Book H — 1 kg 27 g

What is the total weight of books D and H?

1 Find the total weight of Books A and C.

2 Find the total weight of Books D and F.

3 Find the total weight of Books G and H.

4 Find the total weight of the two heaviest books.

5 Find the total weight of the two lightest books.

6 Find the total weight of Books A, B and D.

7 Find the total weight of Books E, F and G.

8 Find the total weight of Books B, C and H.

e**X**tra Find out how much the four heaviest books in your library weigh.
Now make up some questions about their weights for other
children in the class.

Football stadiums

These are the twelve English League Football stadiums with the greatest capacities.

Manchester United	Old Trafford	76 100
Arsenal	Emirates Stadium	60 432
Newcastle United	St James' Park	52 387
Sunderland	Stadium of Light	49 000
Manchester City	City of Manchester	48 000
Liverpool	Anfield	45 362
Aston Villa	Villa Park	42 640
Chelsea	Stamford Bridge	42 449
Everton	Goodison Park	40 569
Leeds United	Elland Road	40 204
Sheffield Wednesday	Hillsborough	39 812
Tottenham Hotspur	White Hart Lane	36 214

Estimate the difference in capacity between each pair of stadiums.

Then find the answer, showing your working. How close were you?

Check your answers using the inverse operation.

1 Old Trafford and Hillsborough

2 Emirates Stadium and Stamford Bridge

3 Anfield and Goodison Park

4 St James' Park and City of Manchester

5 Villa Park and White Hart Lane

6 Stadium of Light and Elland Road

The Union of European Football Associations (UEFA) introduces a new rule that for all night games the capacity of football stadiums must be reduced by 1500 spectators.

7 What will the new capacity be for night games at each of the stadiums?

8 Check all your answers by using the inverse operation.

eXtra Use the internet to find the attendance at a recent home game for each of these football teams. Was the stadium full? How many more people could have fitted in?

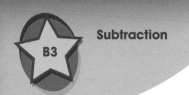

Basketball throws

Eight children measured the distance they could throw a basketball.

Here are their results.

Anwen	12·3 m
Esha	8·56 m
Barney	9 m 26 cm
Faisal	10 m 26 cm
Chandra	7·09 m
Gabby	13 m 20 cm
Dominic	11 m 6 cm
Hassan	6·89 m

What is the difference between Chandra's throw and Gabby's throw?

Change Gabby's throw to a decimal number.
Chandra's throw is 7·09 m. Gabby's throw is 13·2 m.

Now that both throws use the same units it is much easier to find the difference between them.

$$\begin{array}{r} 13{\cdot}20 \\ -7{\cdot}09 \\ \hline \end{array}$$

Using this method, find the difference between these children's throws.
Show your workings.

1 Anwen and Esha

2 Gabby and Hassan

3 Dominic and Barney

4 Faisal and Chandra

5 Dominic and Hassan

6 Faisal and Barney

7 Anwen and Chandra

8 Gabby and Esha

Check your answers using the inverse operation.

eXtra

Write the children's throws in order from longest to shortest. Between which pair of numbers is there the smallest difference?

Probability

Coins

Throw a coin three times. Note if each throw is heads or tails. Do this 50 times.

1 Record your results on the tally chart on PCM 33.

2 Draw a bar graph to show your results.

Based on your results, do you think these markers are in the right positions?
3 Draw markers to show what you have found.

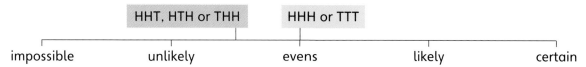

| HHT, HTH or THH | HHH or TTT |

| impossible | unlikely | evens | likely | certain |

Dice

Throw two dice 50 times. Note the total of the two numbers each time.

4 Record your results on the tally chart on PCM 33.

5 Draw a bar graph to show your results.

Based on your results, do you think these markers are in the right positions?
6 Draw markers to show what you have found.

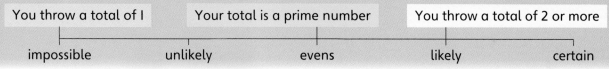

| You throw a total of 1 | Your total is a prime number | You throw a total of 2 or more |

| impossible | unlikely | evens | likely | certain |

Counters

Put 10 counters in a bag: one blue, two red, three yellow and four green.

Take a counter from the bag, note the colour and replace it. Repeat 50 times.

7 Record your results on the tally chart on PCM 33.

8 Draw a bar graph to show your results.

9 Based on your results, do you think these markers are in the right positions?
Draw markers to show what you have found.

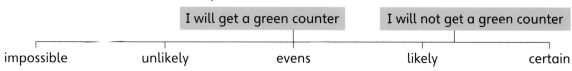

| I will get a green counter | I will not get a green counter |

| impossible | unlikely | evens | likely | certain |

Put a set of 0–9 number cards in a bag. Take a card from the bag, note the number and replace it. Repeat this 50 times. Draw a tally chart of your results. What was the chance of picking an even number? A number bigger than 9? The same number three times in a row? Make up three questions of your own and ask another child in the class to guess the probability.

Weather

Nowadays we use technology to forecast the weather. In the past, people watched for patterns and made up rhymes and sayings to help them predict the weather.

Red sky at night,
Shepherd's delight;
Red sky in the morning,
Shepherd's warning.

If cows are standing in a field it will be fine, but if they are lying down it is going to rain.

Rain before seven, Fine by eleven.

St Swithin's Day if it do rain,
For 40 days it will remain.
St Swithin's Day if it be fair,
For 40 days will rain no more.

St Swithin's Day is on 15th July.

Weather forecasters predict the chance of rain and cloud each day, using evidence that has been collected over a number of years. They compile reports, like this:

Friday 14th November	40% Cloud. Chance of rain 10%.
Saturday 15th November	50% Cloud. Chance of rain 30%.
Sunday 16th November	20%. Cloud. Chance of rain 10%.
Monday 17th November	0% Cloud. Chance of rain 0%.
Tuesday 18th November	60% Cloud. Chance of rain 20%.
Wednesday 19th November	90% Cloud. Chance of rain 100%.
Thursday 20th November	100% Cloud. Chance of rain 60%.

Then they write their weather forecasts using probability information, like this:

Cloud cover	
0%	Clear
10–30%	Mostly clear
40–60%	Partly cloudy
70–80%	Mostly cloudy
90–100%	Cloudy

Possibility of rain	
0% probability	Unlikely
10–20% probability	Slight chance
30–50% probability	Even chance
60–70% probability	Likely
80–90% probability	Very likely
100% probability	Certain

Use this information to write a weather forecast for Friday 14th November to Thursday 20th November. How cloudy will it be? What is the chance of rain?

eXtra

People think that it rains a lot in Britain. Use the internet to find your nearest weather station and note the levels of rain over a year. Write a report explaining whether you agree or disagree with this and why.

The best deal

Saj wants to buy a new phone. He has been shopping around for the cheapest deal and asked two of his friends for advice.

> Jasmine pays a flat rate of 5p per text. Dominic pays 10p per text for the first 50 texts, then 2·5p per text for the next 200 texts and then 10p per text after that.

Saj has plotted the information about his friend's phone deals onto the graph on PCM 34 to help him decide which one to go for.

Use the graph to answer these questions. Show your workings clearly.

1 Which deal is cheaper if Saj only wants to send 50 texts a month?

2 At what point do both deals cost the same? Is there more than one point?

3 Approximately how much does each deal charge for 200 texts?

4 Whose phone deal is cheaper for sending 300 texts?

5 How much does it cost for Dominic to send 400 texts?

6 If Saj only wants to spend £10·00 a month, which is the better deal for him?

   Saj thinks he sends 350 texts a month, but wants to send fewer. If Dominic sends 350 texts he gets 50 of them free.

7 If Saj had Dominic's deal and only sent 300 texts a month, would he save money?

8 Which deal gets more texts for £10?

9 Which deal gets more texts for £20?

10 Use the graph and the answers to the questions above to write a report telling Saj which deal you think is better for him. Explain your reasons fully.

Use the internet to find the costs of some phone deals on offer now. Compare them and discuss with another child in the class which contract would be the best deal to get and why.

Luggage sizes

| Syed | 53·5 cm × 35·5 cm × 195 mm | 11·2 kg |

Syed, Millie, Jake and Farah are going on holiday. They are each going to a different destination and each flying with a different airline.

| Millie | 54·5 cm × 334 mm × 22·5 cm | 18 000 g |

| Jake | 490 mm × 33·5 cm × 20·5 cm | 9000 g |

| Farah | 54·5 cm × 334 mm × 22·5 cm | 6800 g |

Table 1 Airline luggage allowances

Airline	Maximum dimensions	Maximum weight
Flyair	55 × 40 × 20 cm	10 kg
Dashjet	55 × 40 × 20 cm	12 kg
Gobye	50 × 35 × 23 cm	10 kg
BIA	55 × 40 × 23 cm	7 kg
British Jets	56 × 45 × 25 cm	23 kg

1 Look at the size of each case and use the information in Table 1 to work out who is flying with which airline.

In your hand luggage you cannot take any bottle that holds more than 100 ml of liquid and you cannot take more than 1 l of liquid in total.

Table 2 Liquid in hand luggage

	Shampoo	Deodorant	Toothpaste	Cologne	Sun-cream	Water
Syed	33 cl	10 ml	200 ml	150 ml	$\frac{1}{5}$ l	$\frac{1}{2}$ l
Millie	200 ml	20 ml	150 ml	$\frac{1}{10}$ l	100 ml	200 ml
Jake	$\frac{1}{5}$ l	5 cl	10 cl	200 ml	50 ml	100 ml
Farah	150 ml	15 ml	$\frac{1}{3}$ l	0·75 l	0·2 l	$\frac{1}{4}$ l

2 Use Table 2 to work out who has too much liquid in their hand luggage.

3 What should they leave behind so that they can get on the plane?

eXtra Many airlines charge if you want to check in a suitcase and there is a limit to the weight of luggage you are allowed to take on board. Use the internet to find the weight limits of some airlines and if they charge to check a suitcase in. Which airline would you choose to fly with? Why?

Angles and degrees

Early scientists thought that the Sun took 360 days to rotate around the Earth so they decided to divide a circle into 360 units. Today we call these units degrees and use them to measure angles. A full turn has 360 degrees. A right angle has 90 degrees.

Some mathematicians and scientists use measurements smaller than degrees. A degree can be divided into 60 units called minutes. Each minute can be divided into 60 units called seconds.

Making a right-angled triangle without a protractor

Make 14 evenly spaced knots in a length of string.
Pin the first knot to a board and make a four knot ×
five knot × six knot triangle, pinning each corner in place.
Check your right angle with a protractor.

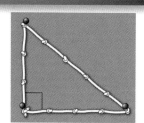

Making a regular pentagon without a protractor

You need a strip of paper 1 cm wide and 20 cm long.
Carefully tie a knot in the paper, keeping it flat. The knot
should form a regular pentagon. Check you have made
a pentagon by measuring the angles with a protractor.

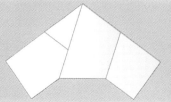

Making an equilateral triangle without a protractor

a Take a piece of A4 paper and fold it in half lengthwise.

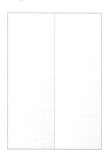

b Fold the bottom left corner up and make a mark where it touches the central fold.

c Unfold the paper and draw a line from the mark to the bottom right corner and the bottom left corner.

d Cut along the lines you have just drawn to make an equilateral triangle.

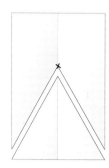

What size will the angles of the triangle be? Check with a protractor.

Use the internet to find out about other units of measurement for measuring angles.

The Shipping Forecast

Have you ever heard the Shipping Forecast?

The Shipping Forecast reports changes in the weather for the seas around the British Isles. It is useful for people who work at sea, such as fishermen, or for people who do water sports such as wind-surfing. The format of the Shipping Forecast is always the same so that people can write the information down quickly.

The information is collected and reports are produced by the UK Meteorological Office for the Maritime and Coastguard Agency.

Since 1949 the waters around the British Isles have been divided up into 'Sea Areas'. The information is given out in order, usually in a clockwise direction starting from the sea area of Viking and finishing at the sea area of Southeast Iceland.

The first forecast for each area is wind direction and speed. The wind direction is the direction that the wind is coming from. The direction of the wind in the Shipping Forecast is given using eight points of the compass. Wind direction can change during the day. The wind is reported as veering if it is moving in a clockwise direction and backing if it is moving in an anticlockwise direction. Wind speed is measured on the Beaufort scale.

If the wind changes from north to east it is **veering** and it has moved clockwise by 90°.
If the wind changes from north to north-west it is **backing** and it has moved anticlockwise 45°.

I   Complete the table on PCM 38, working out which direction the wind has moved from or to and the number of degrees it has moved by.

 e**X**tra   **Find out more about the Beaufort scale for measuring wind speed.**

Interior angles

Each of these shapes is made up of equilateral triangles.

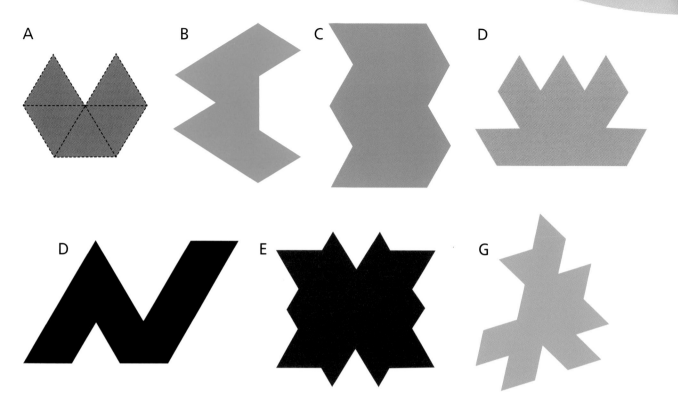

Copy and complete a table like the one below for each shape. Shape A has been done for you.

Count how many interior angles there are and say if they are acute, obtuse or reflex angles. Using what you know about the interior angles of an equilateral triangle, calculate the size of each interior angle and the total of the interior angles.

Type of angle	Number of angles	Size of angle	Total of angles
Acute	2	60°	120°
Obtuse	4	120°	480°
Reflex	I	300°	300°
	Total of interior angles		900°

Use equilateral triangles to make some polygons of your own. Challenge your friends to calculate the total of the interior angles. Calculate the exterior angles of each shape.

Looking at triangles

How many different shaped triangles do you know?

Look at these six triangles.

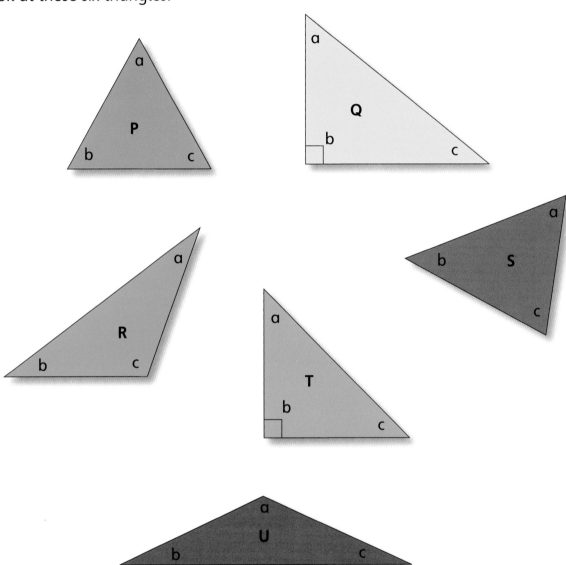

1 What are the properties of each triangle?

2 What is the mathematical name of each triangle?

3 Do you know any other triangles which are not here? Draw them.

eXtra   Which two of the above triangles can be put together edge to edge to make another triangle?

How many are there?

Sweets are packed in nines or tens and there is always one left over.

There are less than 200 sweets all together. How many sweets can there be?

> To solve this problem, we write out all the multiples of 9, adding I each time:
> 10, 19, 28, 37, 46, 55, 64, 73, 82, 91, 100, 109, 118, 127, 136, 145, 154, 163, 172, 181, 190, 199, 208
>
> Then we write out all the multiples of 10, adding I each time:
> 11, 21, 31, 41, 51, 61, 71, 81, 91, 101, 111, 121, 131, 141, 151, 161, 171, 181, 191, 201
>
> Then we check which numbers appear in both lists. There might be more than one. 91 and 181 both appear in this list so the answer is **91** or **181**.

Solve each problem and write out the division calculations to prove your answers.

1 Risha always bakes the same number of cakes. The number is between 20 and 30 cakes. On Monday she groups the cakes into threes and has two left over. On Tuesday she groups them in fours and has three left over. What is the smallest number of cakes she could have baked?

2 The Supermarket sells eggs in boxes of six or ten. They get the same number of eggs each day. The number is between 500 and 550. When the eggs are packed in sixes there are always four left over. When the eggs are packed in tens there are always eight left over. How many eggs does the Supermarket get each day?

3 Andre the builder buys windows for houses he is building. He needs two windows for a small house, three for a medium house and four for a large house. Whichever house he builds, he always has one window left over. What is the smallest number of windows he could have?

4 Daisy makes flower decorations. She buys in the same amount of flowers each day. The number is less than 100. One day she uses five flowers, the next day four flowers and the next six flowers. Each time she has one flower left over. How many flowers could she have bought?

Lucas has three identical packets of biscuits. He gives everyone two biscuits each from the first packet and eats one himself. The next day he gives everyone five biscuits each from the second packet and eats one himself. The day after that he eats one biscuit from the third packet himself then gives everyone seven each. A packet has fewer than 120 biscuits. Exactly how many biscuits are in each packet?

Equivalent calculations

Shuffle the calculation cards from PCM 42 and share them out.

1 Using your chosen method, work out each of the calculations on PCM 42. You can use a mental method, a written method or a calculator.

2 When you have answered the calculations, match each of the calculations on a grey card with three other calculations that have the same answer.

3 What do you notice about each set of calculations? Why do they have the same answer?

4 Adjusting calculations like this can make them easier to work out. Which adjustments make the calculations in the grey boxes easier to work out?

eXtra Find two more equivalent calculations for each of the calculations on the grey cards.

Fractions to decimals

> The decimal equivalent of a fraction can be found by dividing the **numerator** by the **denominator**.
>
> If you use a calculator for this, round your answers to three decimal places.
>
> Example:
> What is the decimal equivalent of $\frac{1}{7}$?
> $1 \div 7 = 0{\cdot}1428571$
> That's **0·143** to three decimal places.

Find the decimal equivalents (to three decimal places) of these fractions.

1 $\frac{1}{6}$ 　　　　2 $\frac{2}{3}$ 　　　　3 $\frac{3}{7}$ 　　　　4 $\frac{5}{8}$

5 $\frac{2}{9}$ 　　　　6 $\frac{5}{6}$ 　　　　7 $\frac{4}{7}$ 　　　　8 $\frac{5}{9}$

Change these pairs of fractions to decimals to find which one is larger.

9 $\frac{4}{9}$ or $\frac{3}{7}$ 　　　　10 $\frac{2}{5}$ or $\frac{3}{8}$ 　　　　11 $\frac{7}{8}$ or $\frac{9}{11}$

12 $\frac{7}{12}$ or $\frac{6}{11}$ 　　　　13 $\frac{15}{17}$ or $\frac{6}{7}$ 　　　　14 $\frac{8}{9}$ or $\frac{18}{19}$

Use this method to put these sets of fractions in order from smallest to largest.

15 $\frac{2}{3}$, $\frac{5}{8}$ and $\frac{4}{7}$ 　　　　　　　　16 $\frac{2}{9}$, $\frac{3}{13}$ and $\frac{1}{6}$

17 $\frac{14}{17}$, $\frac{9}{11}$ and $\frac{11}{13}$ 　　　　　　　18 $\frac{5}{11}$, $\frac{3}{7}$ and $\frac{4}{9}$

 eXtra Find the decimal equivalents of all the fractions with denominators of 7 and denominators of 9. Place these on the 0–1 number line on PCM 43. Order all the fractions with 7 and 9 as denominators to compare sevenths and ninths.

Fruity percentages

How many portions of fruit and vegetables do you eat each day?

Doctors say that we should all eat five portions of fruit and vegetables a day. To help us do this, lots of companies have added fruit juice to their products. You might have seen that there is fruit juice in your yoghurts and sweets, but did you know it can also be found in cereals, and even chocolate?

Some parents think that these products aren't actually healthier. They think that companies add fruit juice just to make us buy the products. They feel that writing 'juice drink' on a low fruit juice product that isn't very good for us shouldn't be allowed. Pure fruit juice contains 100% fruit juice. Some fruit drinks contain as little as 5% real fruit juice. The rest of the drink is made up of water, sugar, sweeteners, flavourings and colourings.

Frugal's Strawberry Fizz contains 12% real fruit.
How much real fruit is there in a:

1 700 ml bottle?   2 250 ml bottle?   3 1·5 litre bottle?

Yogi's Fruit Yoghurt contains 9% real fruit.
How much real fruit is there in a:

4 150 gram pot?   5 400 gram pot?   6 700 gram pot?

Ophrey's Organic Orange Juice contains 35% real fruit.
How much real fruit is there in a:

7 200 ml carton?   8 750 ml carton?   9 1·2 litre carton?

Petra's Pure Prune Juice contains 71% real fruit.
How much real fruit is there in a:

10 800 ml bottle?   11 300 ml bottle?   12 1·4 litre bottle?

eXtra
Use the internet to investigate some fruit drinks.
What percentage of fruit juice do they contain?
How much fruit juice is there in a typical bottle or can?

Ratio and proportion

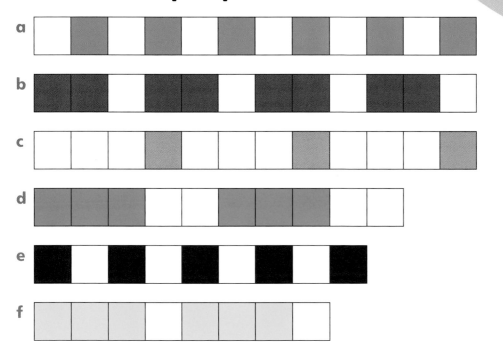

a

b

c

d

e

f

Remember to simplify proportions and ratios.

For each pattern:

1 what proportion of the squares is shaded?

2 what proportion of the squares is unshaded?

3 what is the ratio of shaded squares to unshaded squares?

If the number of squares in each pattern is doubled:

4 how many shaded and how many unshaded squares will there be?

5 what proportion of the squares will be unshaded?

6 what will the ratio of shaded to unshaded squares be?

There are 40 squares in a pattern made up of shaded and unshaded squares. Find the number of shaded and unshaded squares if the ratio of shaded to unshaded squares is:

7 3:5   8 7:1   9 4:6   10 8:2   11 2:3   12 4:1

Make up your own patterns with 20 squares, some shaded and some unshaded. For each pattern, what is the ratio of shaded to unshaded squares? What proportion of the squares is shaded?

Square numbers

1 Copy and complete this table of the square numbers up to 10^2 (10×10).

Number	1	2	3	4	5	6	7	8	9	10
Square	1	4	9							100

Look at the **differences** between consecutive square numbers.

2 Which two square numbers have a difference of 11?

3 Which two square numbers have a difference of 19?

4 Which two square numbers have a difference of 15?

5 Explore the difference between each pair of consecutive square numbers. It might be helpful to draw a table for this. What do you notice?

Use this diagram to explain what you have found.

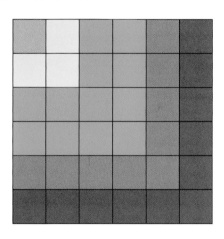

6 Draw a table of the square numbers from 10^2 (10×10) to 20^2 (20×20), and the difference between each pair of consecutive square numbers.

7 Which two square numbers have a difference of 23?

8 Which two square numbers have a difference of 37?

9 Which two square numbers have a difference of 29?

10 Does the pattern for the differences between square numbers continue?

eXtra

Copy and complete this table showing the sum of successive pairs of square numbers.
What pattern do you notice?

Square numbers	$1^2 + 2^2$	$2^2 + 3^2$							$9^2 + 10^2$
Sum	5								

Factors and prime numbers

More about factors

15 has four factors: 1, 3, 5 and 15

1 × 15 = 15   3 × 5 = 15

30 has eight factors: 1, 2, 3, 5, 6, 10, 15 and 30

1 × 30 = 30   2 × 15 = 30   3 × 10 = 30   5 × 6= 30

> If you double any number then that number will always have twice as many factors as the original number.

Look at these pairs of numbers to see if Melanie is right.

1 25 and 50   2 20 and 40   3 12 and 24

4 What did you find? Do you agree with Melanie?

Prime numbers

> A prime number is a number with only two factors, 1 and itself.

5 Why is 2 the only even number which is a prime number?

6 Why isn't 1 considered to be a prime number?

> All numbers ending in 7 are prime numbers.

7 Look at these numbers to see if Bernie is right.

   7   17   27   37   47   57   67   77   87   97

8 What did you find? Do you agree with Bernie?

9 Using the 1–100 number square on PCM 46, cross off all the numbers that are not prime and find all the prime numbers from 1 to 100.

eXtra

Take any prime number and double it. How many factors does the number have? Do you think that this is true for the doubles of all prime numbers? Try with some more prime numbers and describe what you find. Can you explain why this is?

Author team
Jon Kurta
Carol Richardson

Part of Pearson

Ginn is an imprint of Pearson Education Limited, a company incorporated in England and Wales, having its registered office at Edinburgh Gate, Harlow, Essex, CM20 2JE. Registered company number: 872828

www.pearsonschools.co.uk

Ginn is a registered trademark of Pearson Education Limited

Text © Pearson Education Limited 2009

First published 2009

13 12 11 10
10 9 8 7 6 5 4 3

British Library Cataloguing in Publication Data
A catalogue record for this book is available from the British Library

ISBN 978 0 602577 76 6

Typeset by Artistix
Original illustrations © Pearson Education Limited 2009
Illustrated by Matt Buckley, Tom Cole, Jonathan Edwards, Andrew Painter, Anthony Rule, and Q2A.
Cover photo/illustration © Per José Karlén
Printed in China (CTPS/03)

Acknowledgements
The authors and publisher would like to thank the following individuals and organisations for permission to reproduce photographs:
© Fotolia / Rafael Ramirez Lee, Alhambra, p12; © Fotolia / Sandra Henderson, White House, p12; © Shutterstock / Kmiragaya, Houses of Parliament, p12; © Shutterstock / Vinicius Tupinamba, Louvre pyramid, p12; © Alamy / Interfoto Pressebildagentur, Plato, p20; © Bridgeman Art Library / Private Collection, Pope Gregory XIII, p40; © iStockPhoto / XYNO, Julius Caesar, p40; © Corbis / Gianni Dagli Orti, Pythagoras, p43; © Alamy / Mary Evans Picture Library, A. Celsius, p53; © Alamy / Robert Grubba, G.D. Fahrenheit, p53; © Corbis / Christian Llewig, Football stadium, p61.

Every effort has been made to contact copyright holders of material reproduced in this book. Any omissions will be rectified in subsequent printings if notice is given to the publishers.